As I.T. moves to mobile devices,
the cloud, and everything-as-a-service,
MSPs become irrelevant. How can you
provide managed services when there's
nothing left in the data center to manage?

Mark S. A. Smith

From MSP
to BSP

Pivot
from Managed Services Provider
to Business Services Provider
to Profit from I.T. Disruption

{ i

Also by Mark S.A. Smith

Guerrilla Trade Show Selling
Guerrilla TeleSelling
Guerrilla Negotiating
Linux in the Boardroom
Security in the Boardroom
The Accidental Landlord

And many other custom written books and publications for corporate clients.

Published by
The Bija Company, LLC
www.BijaCo.com

v1.1
ISBN 978-1-884059-26-1

Printed in the United States of America.

From MSP to BSP
Pivot from
Managed Services Provider to
Business Services Provider to
Profit from I.T. Disruption

As the world moves to mobile devices, the cloud, and everything-as-a-Service (XaaS), Managed Services Providers (MSPs) become irrelevant. How can you provide managed services when there's nothing left in the data center to manage?

In this pragmatic discourse about the changing role of technology business partners, you learn why this trend accelerates and how to pivot to be a Business Services Provider (BSP), where you work with C-level business executives to implement their roadmap by delivering foresight, management, and protection irrespective of the location or ownership of the technology that runs their company.

Reviews

Mark Smith delineates critical differences between B2C and B2B marketing that technologists must not ignore.

Perry Marshall, Author of 80/20 Sales and Marketing

Anyone who has owned a technology firm knows that you have to reinvent yourself every 5 -7 years to stay current, relevant, and above the commoditization fray. Mark's book is a must read for MSP's who want to continue to survive and thrive in this era of digital transformation.

Linda Rose, Retired Founder and CEO of multiple Microsoft Partner companies

After decades in the I.T. business as founder and CEO of the industry's oldest IT Channel Community, The ASCII Group, it is clear that we are watching the biggest disruption of all time. Some will make it, and those who aren't paying attention, won't. Mark lays out why you must pay attention, what you must do today to make the change, and how to make more profit than ever. Read it. Act on it. Profit from it.

Alan Weinberger, Founder, The ASCII Group

A timely guide for selling in the age of digital transformation. Mark S A Smith's book could not have come at a better time. The 'new' answers to 'what do I do, what do I say, to whom, how, and when' are exquisitely covered in detail. Now it's your turn to take Mark's material, internalize it, execute it, own it, and reach the sales success you deserve.

Marylou Tyler, Co-author, Predictable Prospecting & Predictable Revenue

In business the last thing you need is stability... change presents opportunity and we have never seen such change as is happening in our world today. Everything we "know" is being challenged. Mark has once again applied his experience, observations and incredible insight into a concise toolkit that allows us to understand where in this tsunami of change business opportunity exists. From frictionless transactions through augmented reality the commercialization of space travel and paradigm shift from senior professionals to Millennials. This is gold.

Tony Bulleid, VP Sales Marketing and Operations EMEA

I've never seen our industry in such upheaval as it is. Mark's words are sage advice to those who want to be in it in the future.

Otto E. Coppen, Field Account Executive, Synnex

This book describes the disruption occurring within the I.T. industry. Old business models are evaporating and new business models are proliferating. It then offers sound, practical advice on how sellers can win business in this rapidly changing milieu. If you sell into the I.T. space this book is a must read... for your survival. If you don't sell into the I.T. space read it because it succinctly describes how to sell within a disrupted market.

Thomas J. Williams, Managing Director
Strategic Dynamics Inc.

Now more than ever, it is critical to work ON all of areas of your business, not just IN them. Mark's impactful and actionable insights are a catalyst to do just that!

Mary Ellen Grom, Executive Director,
Marketing Communication, AFL Global

A treasure trove of nuggets! Gold nuggets... Heart of Selling is 90%, Transaction engine vs Trust engine. Mark artfully paves the way towards selling Mission Critical systems. A "must" embrace.

Rajesh Rao, VP Asia Pacific, Viavi Solutions

Well worth the read. Mark points out, don't be just a trusted I.T. advisor. Be the customer's business partner. Work with them to solve their business issues before your competition does. Grow your businesses together. This book shows you how.

Mike Fritzler, Director of Business Development, Powerland, Canada

Disclaimer

Neither the author nor the publisher assumes any responsibility for errors, inaccuracies, or omissions. Any slights of people or organizations are unintentional.

This publication is not intended for use as a source of security, technical, legal, accounting, financial, or other professional advice. If advice concerning these matters is needed, seek the services of a qualified professional as this information is not a substitute for professional counsel.

Neither the author nor the publisher accepts any responsibility or liability for your use of the ideas presented herein. Conversely, neither the publisher nor author will lay claim to any profits you make based on the suggestions of this book.

Some suggestions made in this book concerning business practices may have inadvertently introduced practices deemed unlawful in certain states, municipalities, or countries. You should be aware of the various laws governing your business practices in your particular industry and in your location.

While the Web sites referenced were personally reviewed by the author, there are no guarantees to their safety. Practice safe Internet surfing with current antivirus software and a browser with active security settings.

Dedication

I dedicate this book to all of the I.T. reseller professionals who say, "There's got to be a better way to sell I.T.!" You are the change agents who have the courage to bring disruptive products and services to make the world a better place for all of us.

I dedicate this book to you who practice the Golden Rule – "Do unto others as you would have them do unto you" (Matthew 7:12), which creates lasting, valuable customer relationships and disrupts the competition more than any other idea that I know.

Acknowledgements

I'm grateful to my I.T. reseller colleagues for their ideas, input, and criticism. Whether it was a remark in passing, an axiom in an article, a line from a speech, or a direct "Mark, you need to think about this…" conversation, your thoughts and viewpoints enhance this book. Thanks to you who have "embroidered on my tapestry," adding richness and depth.

Thanks to my clients who let me master how to disrupt as we worked together, especially, Bill Hubler of IBM who hired me to speak to his sales teams over and over again, and Nicole Katrana of IBM who hired me to write dozens and dozens of executive business case assessment tools. Thanks to Chad Czerniak of Arrow Electronics who encourages me to expand my content after more than a decade of collaboration. Thanks to Bob Stegner, Rich Gooding, and William Bailey of Synnex who embraced teaching business acumen to reseller partners.

I thank Brent Green for his insights in the Lifestyle Expression quadrant of the Customer Continuum model, Tony Bodoh for his insights into creating customer experiences that transform profits, Chris Stark for sharing his powerful executive management principles, and Pam Gordon for introducing me to Bruce Joyce's work decades ago. Thank you to Joel Block for his prodigious insights into finance and business models. If I forgot to mention you, it's because we need to talk.

Thanks to my children, Harrison, Christina, Jennifer, Stephen, and Susanna who have taught me the wonders and delights of the Millennial mindset and made me a proud dad.

Heartfelt thanks to my wife, business partner, and best friend, Molly Smith for her unerring wisdom, gentle encouragement, and unending support. Because of her technology industry experience in all parts of the I.T. food chain – reseller, vendor, distributor, and consultant – our consulting business thrives and this book exists.

Special Thanks

Thanks to my early supporters who cheered me on: Brian Cook, Penny Harper, Bill Kerwood, Polly Cook, Capiz Green, Andrew D'Errico, Karyn Buxman, Greg Godek, Brad Hartman, Kim Miller, Matthew Zielsdorf, Bud James, Rolf Strasheim, Craig Kohler, Stephanie Johnson, Mitch Russo, Tony Bulleid, Mary Remon, Steve Shaw, David Hardy, Jane Watson, Stormy Andrews, Trevor Dierdorff, Ryan Swango, Oksana Hansen, Robert Little, John Getter, Kim Nelson, Stacey Naumczik, Martyn Atterton, Gerry Goris, Laura Porreca, Brad Fryer, Meg Jaeger-Blinzler, Bud Kinzer, and Mark DiMassimo.

A special thank you to early reviewers who refined ideas, added valuable comments, and cheered me on: Ed Oakley, Steven Sutton, Linda Rose, Thomas J. Williams, and Victor Pinamonte. Thank you!

Contents

From MSP to BSP
Pivot from
Managed Services Provider to
Business Services Provider to
Profit from I.T. Disruption

Chapter 1:
What's Going On With I.T?

As the world moves to mobile devices, the cloud, and everything-as-a-Service (XaaS), Managed Services Providers (MSPs) become irrelevant.

> HOW CAN YOU PROVIDE MANAGED SERVICES
> WHEN THERE'S NOTHING IN THE DATA CENTER LEFT TO MANAGE?

Shocked by that statement? Good! Stay with me.

In this pragmatic discourse about the changing role of technology business partners, you learn why this trend accelerates and how to pivot to be a Business Services Provider (BSP), where you work with C-level business executives to implement their roadmap by delivering foresight, management, and protection irrespective of the location or ownership of the technology that runs their company.

The Never-ending Changes of Business

As I write this book, the concept of transitioning from a Managed Services Provider to a Business Services Provider is aspirational for many information technology (I.T.[1]) resellers. While I know some have begun the transition to a business-ser-

---

[1] I use periods to denote the difference between I.T. and the word "it" making this book ADA accessible to reading robots.

vices practice, most are still selling servers, storage, and networks, managed services, help desk services, and applications development.

They're hoping to figure out how to stay in business as margins shrink, customers disappear, and new competition comes on the scene. Hope isn't enough. Survival requires a pivot to a new business model.

> HOPE IS NOT AN EFFECTIVE BUSINESS STRATEGY.

I don't expect this book to have a long shelf life. The way I see it, 1,000 days after this book's publication date, either you've made the transformation or you're reading history.

Dealing with shifts in business models isn't easy when you've enjoyed success with your world view and don't yet feel the impact of the future changes. Yet businesses run by supposedly smart people get disrupted all the time. Half of the Fortune 500 list from 2010 no longer exist.

> THE TECH WORLD CHANGES
> FASTER THAN MOST CAN IMAGINE.
> THOSE WHO SELL I.T. MUST STAY AHEAD
> OF THOSE WHO BUY I.T.

Imagine the guys sitting around the blacksmith shop in 1908 watching a Ford Model T putter down the road. "Get a horse!" they taunt, laughing as the driver changes their tire punctured by a horseshoe nail.

Five years later, that blacksmith shop became a filling station and automotive repair shop. [2] A decade later, car tires no

---

[2] Between 1908 and 1927 Henry Ford sold 15 million Model T cars, forever transforming transportation. In the U.S., 200,000 filling stations opened between 1905 and the end of the 1920's.

longer got punctures from the blacksmith's craft as roads became paved and horse traffic disappeared.

Mobile devices, cloud, and XaaS have become our Model T. In the near future, most of our customers won't need a data center, today's equivalent of the blacksmith's forge. Sure, a few vocal customers will scoff, "That won't happen!" Yet historical trends predict otherwise. Get moving or get left behind.

> ## THERE ARE TWO GOOD TIMES TO PIVOT:
> ## LAST YEAR AND TODAY.

I Wrote this for I.T. Sales and Marketing Professionals

I wrote this book for executives who own or direct I.T. sales organizations and vendor executives who rely on the channel to move their merchandise. You've been my tribe for more than 20 years. I've conversed, coached, cajoled, cheered, commiserated, and consumed cocktails with you. I've been working with you thanks to the support of manufacturers and distributors through conferences, training events, video learning systems, webinars, personal conversations, articles, and podcasts.

I've spoken to more than 30,000 members of our community worldwide over the 27 years that I've worked in the world of I.T. sales and marketing. I know what you do, your pain is my pain, your dreams are my dreams.

There's a good probability that you got this book directly from me and are reading it at my urging.

If not, consider this to be my plea for to you to read, consider, pray, decide, and act.[3]

---

[3] I say *pray* because every entrepreneurial business owner believes in a Higher Power, at least during those nights they lay awake pondering, "Dear God, how will I make payroll?"

If this isn't you, you might find it an interesting read that gives you arguing points with your boss or a good reason to go into competition with them.

Sorry, not sorry.

Why Do I Have the Right to Write This?

I trained as an electrical engineer, wrote software, and sold hardware. I've been involved in selling technology since 1982 and run my own company since 1990. Like you, I have wins and losses; trophies, scars, and bruises.

We entrepreneurial technologists are people of passion. We love knowing how things work, solving problems, and making the world a better place. We whole-heartedly care about the success of our family, our employees, our customers, our community, and the technology we bring to them. We think about this business more than anything else. It's our identity and it's our drive. I love you… yes, you… too much to see your heart-felt business crash and burn.

Let's take this thing to a new level of purpose and success. Are you in?

My Motivation for Writing This

Massive disruptors (that we'll discuss) accelerate the changes in I.T., which alter forever the business. These influences converge into an unstoppable tsunami, wiping out those who refuse to take the high ground and lifting to higher levels of profitability those who can surf the sea change. I'll lay out for you what I predict as the most probable roadmap to success.

I've been watching the I.T. world slowly pivot away from selling hardware to selling services. That trend accelerates at break-neck pace.

You can't run a business selling computer hardware that gets refreshed every three to five years at single-digit margins. You can't afford to sell software for a few points while the vendor takes all the recurring maintenance revenue. You can't sell managed services at ever-decreasing hourly rates. It's a race to the bottom. You can't build a sustainable, scalable, profitable or salable business in this environment.

> ## THE MSP BUSINESS IS NOW A RACE TO THE BOTTOM.

Compound this with ever-increasing vendor "enablement" requests, frantically expecting you to learn more about their technology as sales numbers drop and executives demand action. You could fill your calendar with "MUST ATTEND" events.

Yet, without a clear and immediate business benefit, you can't afford to take days away from calling customers to attend distributor conferences and vendor trainings, view webinars and read product manuals.

Besides, that knowledge becomes worthless in 12 to 18 months as Moore's Law[4] obsoletes your knowledge. Technical knowledge loses its attraction when there's so many other business demands. It's just not worth it.

> ## MOORE'S LAW MEANS YOUR PRODUCT KNOWLEDGE BECOMES WORTHLESS NEXT YEAR.

How to Get the Most Out of This Book

Because of all this, you might be feeling burnt out, tired, and discouraged. Hang in there. I wrote this book to bring you a fresh, new vision.

I designed this book to be read on an airplane flight.[5] You should be able to get the key points and relevant ideas in 60 minutes or less. You'll notice there aren't dense blocks of text because executives learn in short chunks. Scan through, read

---

[4] https://en.wikipedia.org/wiki/Moore%27s_law
[5] I wrote most of it on airplane flights.

the headings and memes, stop and dig in where your attention goes.

You may notice some intentional minor repetition as you read because I want a skimming reader to get the idea in context without having to read from beginning to end.

Then take time to digest, debate, question, consider, adapt, and ultimately pivot your team to a new future vision.

Here's a few ways to get the most from your investment in reading this.

Unlearn and Learn

Are you willing to unlearn and relearn? This requires you to suspend judgement to see the big picture and then decide what will be right for you and your team.

> "IN TIMES OF CHANGE,
> LEARNERS INHERIT THE EARTH,
> WHILE THE LEARNED FIND THEMSELVES
> BEAUTIFULLY EQUIPPED TO DEAL WITH A WORLD
> THAT NO LONGER EXISTS." – ERIC HOFFER

Use this book to help you unlearn and learn. Underline phrases, circle paragraphs, fold down pages, make notes. A pristine book doesn't work as well as one marked up and mutilated. Don't worry, you can get another copy for your archives.

The bad news: most of what you and your team know won't work in the future.

The good news: your business experience is your most valuable asset.

I'm going to push you out of your comfort zone. Will you be okay with me challenging you? Can you handle the truth when you observe it?

If not, save yourself some grief and put this book down.

If so, let's go!

> AS TECHNOLOGY ACCELERATES,
> THE FUTURE BELONGS TO THOSE
> WHO CAN UNLEARN FASTEST.

Boldly Go Where You Haven't Been

You have to be able to think about a future that doesn't yet exist that you'll create using methods you haven't yet experienced nor invented.

This requires courage to focus on the strategic and objective *what* you're going to do and motivational *why* you're doing it without knowing the tactical *how* you'll do it.

Can you stay focused on the new vision in the face of doubt and uncertainty of how you'll get it done?

> "STORM YOUR OWN GATES OR OTHERS WILL."
> – CHRIS STARK

Lead Though the Chaos

You have to be willing to fearlessly lead your team through some massive changes in expertise, sales methodology, delivery systems, and compensation plans. Not all of your beloved team will make the transition.

Will you be okay letting go of some of your seasoned team?

What to Expect

The future of I.T is a moving target and we have to surf the chaos to create a business that is sustainable, scalable, profitable, and ultimately, salable.

Some of what you'll read, you already know, and I ask you to think about it in a new way.

Some of the things you'll discover, you used to do, and I'll remind you that it's time to do them again.

And, without a doubt, I've got new ideas for you. When you choose to use them, you can be as successful as you wish. Are you ready for the transformation?

Chapter Summary

❑ Disruptive forces rock traditional I.T. business models and threaten Managed Services Provider's livelihood.

❑ This requires a change in business models to survive and thrive.

❑ It requires a willingness for the business executive to explore strategy and tactics that haven't been used before.

Ask Yourself

❑ What have I noticed about the changes in my business?

❑ Considering the future of my business, what are the biggest challenges I face? Is it people, process, politics, capital, infrastructure, intellectual property, data analysis, or something else?

❑ How much longer do I want to be in business? Is it worth it to make the pivot?

❑ Am I willing to invest my time and energy to pivot my business to exploit the new business realities?

Ask Your Team

❑ What changes do we need to make to be relevant to our customers and become more valuable to our target market?

❑ What would it be worth for us to do that?

❑ Can you make the changes necessary for us to pivot to the new I.T. sales realities?

Action Plan

❑ Keep reading.

❑ Mark up this book, take notes, bend over pages.

❑ Determine who else need to read this. Buy them a copy and give it to them.

Chapter 2:
What's Causing
Massive I.T. Disruption?

Information Technology morphs, yet again, to the next phase of existence, transitioning from data being location-specific – accumulated, aggregated, analyzed, and served on systems of the customer's design – to data becoming fluid and functional – data flowing in many forms from many locations, accumulated and animated to deliver insights and prompt decisions more rapidly, accurately, and more resourcefully.

> IN A RAPIDLY CHANGING WORLD,
> IT'S NOT ABOUT CONSENSUS BUT ABOUT MAKING DECISIONS
> IN THE ABSENCE OF CERTAINTY
> BECAUSE ABOUT THE TIME YOU GAIN AGREEMENT,
> THE OBJECTIVE HAS CHANGED.

The traditional data center is going away and it won't come back. Let's explore the fundamental reasons why.

Technology Change Outstrips Organization's Ability to Change

Technology changes exponentially (doubling in capability and value every 12 to 18 months, observed by Moore's Law and Metcalfe's Law[6]) while organizations change logarithmically (compound increases of annual growth with the rate declining over time).

---

[6] https://en.wikipedia.org/wiki/Metcalfe%27s_law

Scott Brinker dubbed this observation Martec's law in 2013.[7] He noted that management must strategically choose which changes to deploy because traditional business organization can't handle too much change.

In time, the gap widens until the organization is forced into a drastic reset, gets acquired, or closes. See graphic below.[8]

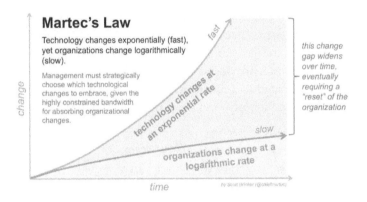

Martec's Law Describes Organizational Resets
Driven by Technology

We haven't had a mass technology reset since 2000. Remember Y2K? Let's observe Martec's Law in action.

Digital Disruption Tanks Big Companies

What is digital disruption? Any data technology that isn't housed in the data center disrupts traditional I.T.: high-speed cellular networks, cloud compute and storage, big data, mobile compute devices, the API economy, everything-as-a-service,

---

[7] http://chiefmartec.com/2013/06/martecs-law-technology-changes-exponentially-organizations-change-logarithmically/
[8] Graphic used with permission.

Internet-of-things, artificial intelligence, virtual reality, augmented reality, e-commerce, blockchain, cryptocurrency, 3D printing, social media, search engines, and way more.

In April 2017, Information Age magazine predicted, "Forty percent of the Fortune 500 won't exist in 10 years because they won't survive digital disruption."[9]

My informal polls support this future vision. I think the estimate understates the number of failures because I expect lots of merger and acquisition activity as major companies falter and can't or don't make the transformation because of lack of vision, lack of knowhow, or run out of resources to pivot.

> "COMPANIES ARE NO LONGER COMPETING AGAINST EACH OTHER.
> THEY ARE COMPETING AGAINST SPEED."
> – MARC BENIOFF, CEO, SALESFORCE.COM

This hypothesis gains support by the work of Clayton M. Christensen, who more than two decades ago wrote his seminal book, *The Innovator's Dilemma*.[10] He observed that companies rarely survive technology transitions because they can't internally and politically keep up with the changes required. He explored why and outlined how to survive.

I recommend that you read the recently updated version after you finish this book.

Disappearing Data Centers

Mark Hurd, CEO of Oracle, proclaims, "Eighty percent of corporate data centers will be gone by 2025. The change will not be linear but exponential. Eighty percent of I.T. funding goes to

---

[9] http://www.information-age.com/65-c-suite-execs-believe-four-ten-fortune-500-firms-wont-exist-10-years-123464546/
[10] http://amzn.to/2wPQLqI

maintenance, twenty percent to innovation. That will reverse."[11]

> ## "EIGHTY PERCENT OF DATA CENTERS WILL BE GONE BY 2025."
> ## – MARK HURD, CEO, ORACLE

Do you agree with this prediction? In my informal poll of hundreds of I.T. reseller owners, engineers, and sales professionals, almost all agree this is highly probable.

As a result, we lose our tried-and-true CIO[12] contacts when companies move away from deploying their own I.T. in their on-site data centers. This disrupts the I.T. sales process, distribution, and managed services as we know them today.

If true, 80 percent of your customers will go away if you expect to sell traditional I.T.: servers, storage, networks, security, services, and applications.

Can your current business model survive an 80 percent reduction in potential customers?

I didn't think so.

It gets worse.

At-Capacity Corporate Data Centers Means There's Nowhere to Go But the Cloud

Think about your mid-market customers. What percentage of their data centers are near or at capacity: racks full, no more power or cooling available?

If you're like others I've polled, you'll find that between 50 and 80 percent of data centers have no room. This trend was first documented in 2007 when 43 percent of 600 data centers

---

[11] https://blogs.wsj.com/cio/2017/01/17/oracle-co-ceo-mark-hurd-says-80-of-corporate-data-centers-gone-by-2025/

[12] I refer to the head of I.T. as the chief information officer (CIO). This role can also be filled by the chief technology officer (CTO).

surveyed were at capacity, driven by power and cooling demands of new blade server installations.[13] And it's only gotten worse.

> ### WHEN YOUR DATA CENTER IS FULL, CLOUD LOOKS VERY ATTRACTIVE.

Here's the problem: 50 to 80 percent of your customers can't buy from you, even if they want to, because they've got no place to put it.

Given that customers spend $100,000 to $300,000 per rack to build out new data centers, it may be too expensive for the board of directors to agree to a new facility given there are other options.[14]

The CIO's hands are tied. The only place to go is the cloud.

When that occurs, your business model gets disrupted and you can completely lose customer control: what are you going to manage?

Mass Retirement of I.T. Execs

The average tenure of US CIOs is around 4.5 years.[15] They don't have much time in which to implement change.

Further complicating the future, you'll see mass retirements of senior I.T, staff in the next 6 to 18 months. You may have already observed the beginning of this trend. Many would have retired sooner but with the crash of 2009 couldn't

---

[13] http://www.datacenterdynamics.com/capacity-crisis-data-centers-running-out-of-space-and-are-on-power-overload/29830.fullarticle

[14] http://www.thecloudcalculator.com/calculators/build-vs-buy.html

[15] https://www.forbes.com/sites/oracle/2016/01/20/oracle-ceo-hurd-hammers-on-economic-themes

because of the decimation of their 401K retirement funds. With Wall Street at record levels, they're cashing out.

This turnover triggers a massive change in culture, corporate knowledge, and strategy. Along the way, I.T. purchase decisions go on hold until they retire. They're not going to agree to a risky purchase that might tarnish their career.

Who's going to replace them?

Here comes the Millennial generation who view I.T. through a radically different lens. Do you have a relationship with those who will soon be taking over the data center? If not, your business is at risk.

Ideally, the change in CIO will mean a positive change in corporate structure. Traditionally, the CIO reported to the CFO because computers were used to implement the company's accounting and bookkeeping systems. Today, I.T. is the business engine, so the CIO must report to the COO, just like manufacturing, facilities, and other operations functions.

From Paying for Ownership to Paying for Access

Millennials challenge traditional Baby Boomer values. We now move from the age of ownership – and a fear of loss – to the age of access – and a fear of missing out (FOMO).[16]

When you can change your mind with a month's notice, you start to look for other, better options. FOMO drives this behavior. If you feel this incites chaos, you'd be correct. And it's inevitable.

Let's look at some examples of values shifting from paying for ownership to paying for access.

You may have noticed that we no longer buy, instead we rent or subscribe. We don't buy movie DVDs, we Netflix them. We don't buy CD recordings, we get Spotify or Apple Music. Millennials own cars in substantially fewer numbers as prior generations because they Uber.

---

[16] Thank you, Tony Bodoh for this brilliant insight.

Home ownership is at record lows. Millennials defer buying a house by seven years as compared with earlier generations, preferring to rent, cohabitate, or live with their parents. Granted, this is driven by a high level of student debt preventing them from being able to make major purchases.[17] When they do buy, they often skip a starter house and opt for a larger, more luxurious home.

This world view extends to the data center. Why would one buy, own, maintain, power and cool, and dispose of something one can purchase as a utility with cloud?

> MILLENNIALS WANT A DATA CENTER TO BE AS EASY TO BUY, DEPLOY, AND MANAGE AS THEIR SMART PHONE.

We're changing business models from a focus on the efficiency of ownership to the flexibility of monthly payments. More about this shift on page 45.

Exponential Data Growth

According to IBM's, *10 Key Marketing Trends For 2017*, 90 percent of the world's data has been created in the last two years, at 2.5 quintillion bytes a day. With more mobile devices, Internet of things (IoT), and more data generating technologies emerging, the growth rate accelerates.[18]

If you want to grow your business, find customers with rapid data growth. The faster the growth, the less likely they are to keep up with the data onslaught and the associated management and curation.

---

[17] http://www.businessinsider.com/millennial-homeownership-lower-2017-6

[18] https://www-01.ibm.com/common/ssi/cgi-bin/ssi-alias?htmlfid=WRL12345USEN

What's Driving Data Growth

Consider these sources of rapidly growing data:

❑ Virtual machines and virtual desktops demand huge amounts of data storage and bandwidth.

❑ Billions of mobile devices, machine-to-machine (M2M) data exchange, and ubiquitous IoT sensors all generate massive data traffic.

❑ Video everywhere for security, conferences, education, and training demands bandwidth, low latency, and massive storage.

❑ Augmented and virtual reality requires a low-latency network and lots of compute power.

❑ Disaster recovery and business continuity demands double or triple the required infrastructure.

❑ Increasing compliance, e-discovery, and archive mandates call for data to remain on-line, searchable, and rapidly available, increasing the amount of data that must be stored, secured, and curated.

❑ With email and file attachments, there's lots of duplication and little gets deleted.

❑ In law enforcement, car and body cameras become critical evidence requiring chain of custody management.

Data overwhelms your customers and they can barely keep up. They need your help.

Consumer Tech Disrupts the Data Center

Artificial intelligence (AI), augmented reality (AR), and natural language programming (NLP) shake the traditional information technologies to the core. These services demand massive bandwidth, compute power, and generate huge data sets, putting even more strain on the creaky infrastructure.

5G and future mobile technology change network topology and so expand how and where data services get created and consumed. High speed bandwidth everywhere opens new data vistas yet to be imagined.

Augmented Reality Disrupts Break/Fix

Augmented reality overlays digital information on live scenes, expanding and enhancing the information and experience. Early examples of that are the computer-generated first down markers you see on televised football games and the geo search game, Pokémon Go and Harry Potter Go.

This brings serious disruption to the world of break/fix.

Expert DIY I.T. Repair

Imagine a troubleshooting customer pointing their mobile phone at an I.T. equipment rack. The camera image processed by the AI engine recognizes the configuration, assisted by RFID and GPS coordinates.

The malfunctioning server glows from the AR overlay of the 3D space. Moving around to the back of the rack, the wires that need to be removed from the server glow. Touch the wrong wire and a warning alert flashes. Remove and open the server, guided by video example overlay, and the broken component glows.

Under the watchful tutelage of artificial intelligence, guided by the augmented reality, the customer replaces the board shipped out from the Amazon warehouse an hour ago.

The customer reconnects the server with AI insuring the right wires get matched to the right ports. The troubleshooting app triggers a diagnostic and declares the trouble resolved.

This isn't a dream. It's currently under development with many tech vendors.

> AI AND VR LETS LOW SKILLED WORKERS EXECUTE BETTER BREAK/FIX THAN YOUR BEST TECH.

With AI and AR, a minimum wage employee can do the work of a $250/hour tech, faster, cheaper, and more reliably.

Expect for most break/fix opportunities to go away. If you're not fixing things as a matter of course, how can you be a managed services provider?

What's the Opportunity?

The future of business data is a mixture of rented and owned technology, data sources, and applications plumbed together forming a unique system that delivers agile business outcomes, based on ever-changing business rules to a consumer base consuming services that deliver a frictionless experience.

> "RESULTS ARE OBTAINED BY EXPLOITING OPPORTUNITIES, NOT BY SOLVING PROBLEMS."
> – PETER F. DRUCKER

Where does this leave our tech community? Where does this leave our distribution partners? Where does this leave you?

Somebody has to assess, align, architect, and interconnect this conglomeration of hardware, data sources, applications, services, and value-added networks. It might as well be you.

The skills required to do this require business acumen and strategic design, not technology acumen and tactical architecture. Ultimately, we must teach our customers how to manage, mine, and monetize their data to accomplish their mission.

How Do We Deal with This?

In this book, I'll discuss the future of data, taking into consideration who cares about data and who doesn't, critical to target marketing, relationship management, and performance analysis. I'll identify other factors driving the I.T. transition and how to connect evolving business roadmaps to new vendor technology roadmaps to craft a tight, long-term, profitable business partnership.

We'll develop new sales strategies, compensation models, and deployment approaches that have the flexibility and depth to manage technology shifts, most of which we can't yet even imagine. We look at how I.T. sales must shift from low-consideration tactical methods to high-consideration strategic assessments, changing the sales game and the business demands on reseller organizations.

And we'll plan how you can be positioned to take clear advantage of the rapid changes that are in the foreseeable future, bringing the right mix of vendors, insights, tools, strategies, tactics, and business acumen.

Shall we do this together?

Chapter Summary

❑ With the increasing gap between the technology available and the technology used by many companies, a massive digital disruption looms, with a substantial percentage of companies unlikely to make the transition.

❑ The I.T. goods and services you provide today lose value rapidly. It's time to pivot to provide customers with more sustainable value.

❑ Your traditional I.T. customer relationships are beginning to disappear. This accelerates to the point that 80 percent won't exist in the next five to seven years.

❑ Massive shifts in cultural values change what the next generation of I.T. professionals find valuable and will commit to. You'll need to pivot to provide what they'll pay for.

Ask Yourself

❑ What do I see as the rapidly accelerating changes in my customer's attitudes?

❑ Do I believe that these trends will continue?

❏ Am I willing to embrace the new cultural values that drive the changes in technology deployment strategy?

❏ What changes do I need to make in my team to adapt to this inevitable future?

Ask Your Team

❏ Are our traditional customers talking about retiring?

❏ Who do you think will replace our contacts? Do we have relationships with them?

❏ How big is the technology gap within our customer base?

❏ How at-risk is our business as these changes expand?

Action Plan

❏ Identify the technology gaps in your own business. Where do you need to up level your technology?

❏ Ask all of your CIO customers, "I'm noticing that many I.T. leaders are announcing plans to retire. Is this in your near future?"

❏ Ask to be introduced by those retiring to higher level executives so that you can develop a customer succession plan.

❏ Develop relationships with the CIO heirs apparent to preserve the account.

Chapter 3:
All Business Models Pivot

The source of funding and on-going revenue determines an operation's business model. Models vary depending if the investment comes from Wall Street, venture capital, angel investors, or friends, family, and fools. The business model depends on if revenue comes from taxes, tuition, transactions, subscriptions, or donations. As time passes, what's considered valuable, worthwhile, and profitable changes, forcing a re-engineering of the organization's business model.

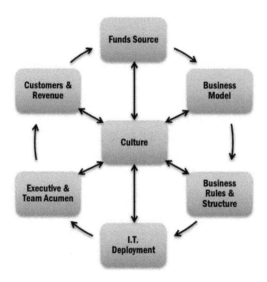

The Business Model Cycle

Here's how the business model cycle works: the source of funds determines the business model, which is defined by business rules and corporate structure, which get implemented through I.T. systems, which support and augment executive and team business acumen and operations, which determines who does business with the company and how much they buy, which rewards the source of funds with a return on investment.

A business model determines the required level of the team skill and executive acumen. The I.T. deployment can automate and enforce business rules, and can broker exceptions. For example, a fast food restaurant model allows unskilled workers to crank out the food and take money, but they can't refund money without a manager override. A franchise owner licenses a proven business model that doesn't require them to have experience or acumen in that market. As long as they follow the process, there's a high probability of success.

Conversely, a business model that requires a high degree of team and executive cognitive capacity – such as specialized consulting (legal, medical, technology) – may not be highly scalable without artificial intelligence defining the business rules.

> EVERY ORGANIZATIONAL CULTURE PROMOTES BLIND SPOTS THAT INADVERTENTLY CAUSE THEIR BUSINESS TO ULTIMATELY FAIL. INNOVATION COMES FROM ELIMINATING THOSE BLIND SPOTS.

All of this centers around the organization's culture, which can be set by the business model, and which can override any of the business model elements. Get the culture right and everything in the model flows. Get it wrong and culture will break the business model.

> IN EVERY BUSINESS, THE SOURCE OF FUNDS DICTATES THE BUSINESS MODEL AND CULTURE DICTATES SUCCESS.

While defining and managing culture is beyond the scope of this book, understanding its impact on business models and resulting business success brings maturity to business model development.

Wall Street Drives Business Models

Wall Street drives publicly-traded company business models. Investors reward certain models with stock valuation increases beyond expected earnings per share ratios, so corporate executives select models most likely to raise the value of their stock.

The biggest valuation lever today: moving from transactional revenue to recurring revenue because stock valuations typically increase by two to six times when you do. We've seen even higher multiples with Amazon and other business unicorns (Uber, Snapchat, Instagram, etc.). If your company doesn't generate recurring revenues, investors aren't interested. This effect drives every modern business model pivot.

> THE BIG BUSINESS MODEL SHIFT: RECURRING REVENUE.

When building recurring revenue, the strategy shifts to one that commoditizes transactional competitors and creates unique value through continuous focus on customer outcomes.

Business Rules Implement Business Models

Business models get installed in an organization through business rules. Need to change the model? Change the rules.

Rule changes often demand changes to I.T. infrastructure, data flow, and decision trees. New rules change the information required by executives to drive the business and change how customers interact. The more dynamic the business model, the more dynamic the changes in business rules, challenging traditional I.T. architecture inflexibility.

Let's consider the impact of new business models and rules for the four main players in the I.T. ecosystem: vendors, distributors, resellers, and customers.

Vendor Business Model Transformation

You'll find virtually all I.T. vendors and manufacturers listed on a stock exchange. It's how they can fund a capital-intensive business and how the founders cash out. Therefore, virtually all vendors are in some stage of pivoting to recurring revenue models with profound impact on their business and operations and how they expect to do business with you.

From Selling Transactions to Building Recurring Revenue Relationships

Moving from building widgets that sell as a SKU (stock keeping unit) to a subscription or metered service radically changes product strategy, marketing metrics, and sales tactics.

Instead of selling to customers every three to five years, as was the norm pre-Y2K, and counting on general business growth for incremental revenues, vendors engineer new ways to deliver subscription and utility-like services. Some customers willingly embrace this shift and others resist.

Vendors can't drive technology innovation too far because most customers can't tolerate revolutionary change, preferring the security of minor incrementalism found in dot releases of software (i.e., V2.1) instead of full version revisions (i.e., V3.0).[19]

Want to prove this to yourself? What percentage of your customers still run Windows 7?

I rest my case.

------

[19] More than a few vendors have experienced this problem. Go-to-market solutions to this exist, which are beyond the scope of this book. If this is you, let's talk.

From Designing Products to Architecting Platforms

The pivot required shifts from designing point-function products to architecting platforms that host the functions, connect with associated technologies, and deliver customer outcomes.

A great example of a platform is the smart phone. By delivering a flexible, application-defined information access system with constant connectivity, what was once a telephone becomes our constant companion, help mate, and business enablement tool.

The smart phone becomes the platform for everything that we expect from technology, completely self-tailored to the user's whim, with vendors collecting fees along the way for delivering value to an ever-changing customer base.

> I DON'T KNOW WHY WE CALL THEM PHONES,
> IT'S THE FUNCTION I USE LEAST.

For I.T, cloud, hyper-converged systems, and XaaS provide the flexible platforms on which customers build their agile business models.

Frankly, the hardware platforms don't much matter anymore. There's no room in the market for new server manufacturers, given that the biggest cloud players manufacture their own based on open hardware platforms. The traditional hardware players consolidate as Broadcom, IBM, and other players, exit the hardware market one product line at a time. Expect this trend to expand beyond servers to all I.T. infrastructure.

From Pitching Closed, Proprietary Products to Joining Community-Based, Open Systems

In a platform-based world, you have to play well with others because you can't effectively satisfy all customers' value demands on your own. Nor do you want to, it's not profitable.

Mass marketing made sense in the past when a factory stamped out millions of identical widgets. Today, buyers demand customized products for even simple purchases. The community drives product marketing, abandoning mass marketing for target-, affinity-, and identity-based marketing. For vendors to stay relevant, they must move from efficiency to flexibility because that's what the market demands.

For example, the $20,000 Coca-Cola® Freestyle® machine allows consumers to mix their favorite beverage flavors in 146 combinations. Although the cost per serving is 30 percent more than ordinary soda fountains, no one seems to care. The data gathered from these machines allows the Coca-Cola Company to determine which flavors to mass market, already knowing what will be a winner. Next flavor up, Cherry Sprite®. In this case, the delivery platform improves product relevance and market success.

> CONSUMER TECHNOLOGY NOW SETS THE BAR
> FOR INFORMATION TECHNOLOGY.

The Adidas® Speedfactory annually manufactures 500,000 individually unique pairs of Futurecraft© shoes using 3D printing and advanced manufacturing techniques, serving hundreds of fashion and passion niches. In a politically-correct move, this brings manufacturing from China back to the local country.

Incoming CIOs expect for technology vendors to provide this same level of integration, customization, and invention.

From a business value standpoint, smaller market segments now have more profits and less competition than mass market segments. While there's more of them, they're easier to manage, track, and serve in a meaningful way.

The bottom line, vendors want to sell subscriptions. How will your business model pivot to take advantage of this?

Distributor Business Model Transformation

Value added distributors (VADs) have made their fortunes from stocking and financing products. They provide the logistics, reverse logistics, financing, billing, and management of channel sales forces, using economies of scale to bring new products to market for smaller companies, and leveling out sales and inventory swings for large ones.

In the past, sales enablement focused on product education: all about speeds and feeds, cables and bays, trays and arrays, product specs and PowerPoint® decks. That's not sales enablement, that's product training.

With less technical knowledge required to sell and deploy subscription-based systems, sales enablement becomes more about how customers extract value from the product (manage, mine, monetize) instead of how the product works. With fewer products to stock and ship, and the pivot to platforms and systems education, how does all of this fit together?

From Systems Architecture to Systems Orchestration

The conversation shifts away from system architecture because AI will assess and work through those details. The new focus rests on system orchestration: connecting mobile devices, IoT devices, XaaS, value-added networks, on-site compute, cloud services, and external data sources.

> THERE'S LESS FOCUS ON THE PUZZLE PIECES
> AND MORE FOCUS ON BUILDING THE PICTURE.

From Vendor Line Card Ranking to Vendor Collaboration Ranking

A popular vendor success metric is the Gartner Magic Quadrant, which examines a vendor's ability to innovate and execute. Those in the Magic Quadrant can do both.

The Golden Quadrant

Expect a new vendor success metric: The Golden Quadrant, identifying a vendor's ability to innovate and collaborate. An extension of the Golden Rule — treat other's systems and data like you would treat your own — those in the Golden Quadrant play well with others inventing new configurations and outcomes versus insisting on their proprietary platform. Add this metric along with distributor vetting of vendor credibility, viability, road map innovation, and investment, and you'll have a solid guide on who to choose as your technology partner.

The Golden Quadrant:
Vendors Delivering High Innovation and High Collaboration

Low innovation and low collaboration, the Lead quadrant, describes the common misalignment of vendor and buyer collaboration. Low innovation and high collaboration, the Brass quadrant, represents traditional consulting engagements, which can only innovate so far. High innovation and low collaboration, the Silver quadrant, identifies a traditional vendor relationship. The Golden Quadrant is where buyers and sellers have open, innovative collaboration to jointly create new processes, inventions, and greater value for all involved.

> CUSTOMERS NO LONGER BUY THE
> "ONE THROAT TO CHOKE" PITCH.
> THEY EXPECT EVERYONE TO PLAY WELL TOGETHER.

Resellers will choose the Golden Quadrant vendors who exhibit flexibility and take responsibility for integration of multiple participants. If you can't play well with others, customers will ignore you.

From Product Financing to Business Systems Financing

The big VAD value-add becomes financing and leasing. Traditionally, most will finance entire I.T. deployments. They'll do deals that are way too complex for banks. They have a higher risk tolerance for financing technology, understanding how to manage and mitigate business risk because they know how to reclaim and dispose of I.T. products.

> FLEXIBLE AND INCLUSIVE FINANCING
> BECOMES A KEY VAD VALUE PROPOSITION.

The bottom line: expect the prime function of VADs in the future to be I.T. finance, data risk insurance, centers for vendor collaboration, and organizing I.T. reseller communities.

Partner Business Model Transformation

With all of the other players pivoting, it's only natural that I.T. resellers must pivot. Over the past decade, partners have transitioned from peddling gear to providing managed services. Ready for the next pivot?

From Product Acumen to Business Acumen

I.T. resellers must pivot from technology acumen to business acumen. You'll need to understand your customer's business almost as well as the CEO and COO to help them design, deploy, and re-deploy the technology that runs their operation.

> MORE BUSINESS VALUE COMES FROM
> CUSTOMER EXPERTISE THAN FROM PRODUCT EXPERTISE.

The data center executive who doesn't have the know how nor have the motivation to embrace business acumen loses their position of power. One example of this today: the marketing department specifies and buys more I.T. than the data center. The data center executive is often left in the cold because of their unwillingness to consider newer technologies and rapid deployment scenarios.

The good news: it's easier to acquire business acumen than I.T. product acumen. You'll always have the distributor and vendor subject matter experts available when it's time to discuss technology.

Fit the Technology Roadmap to the Customer Roadmap

Your value comes from your ability to discuss your customer's business roadmap and help them design, orchestrate, protect, manage, educate, and innovate technology to deliver their business vision.

This means you're much better off hiring sales people with business acumen than tech acumen. More about this on page 135.

From Hardware Deployment to Systems Deployment

With less hardware to deploy, you'll be identifying, organizing, and documenting customer business rules. You'll review, vet, select, plumb, and protect the data paths regardless of the technology location. You'll work with the data creators and data consumers to design and deploy their systems instead of just working with the data curators in the data center. More about this on page 45.

Ultimately, you'll become an extension of the customer's operating expense (OpEx), part of their monthly operating costs, just like rent, utilities, and insurance. You'll be present at every customer strategic initiative conversation because you're the business rules implementation expert.

From Product Sales Compensation to Customer Success Compensation

Traditionally, you've compensated your sales teams on a percentage of gross margin from the successful execution of a hardware and software purchase order. And they've done well.

The days of these large purchases and commensurate commission checks are about over. You'll need to switch to a different sales compensation model. More about this on page 162.

Expect your compensation to be some form of revenue sharing with customers. You'll get a fee for providing your services and progressive companies will provide a share of their revenues with you.

The bottom line: your business changes radically while profits substantially increase. We'll explore in detail the business model pivots required starting with Chapter 4.

Customer Business Model Transformation

We've experienced a radical shift in consumer expectations driven by mobile devices, the Internet, and social media.

MARKET WINNERS DELIVER
A FRICTIONLESS EXPERIENCE
TO PASSIONATE CUSTOMERS.

Customers want everything right now. They want a frictionless customer experience as delivered by Uber for transportation, by Amazon 1-Click for every imaginable purchase, by Netflix for entertainment, and by voice command by Alexa, Cortana, and Siri.

These shifts demand new approaches to I.T. deployment. We used to travel to an office to work because that's where the network to the data center terminated and where the landline phone attached to our desks.

Now IP telephones route calls to where we happen to be, and more and more people just carry a mobile phone. With the elimination of long-distance phone bills, your area code no longer indicates anything other than where you first bought your mobile phone.

> WE NO LONGER GO TO WORK, WE JUST DO WORK.

We can access virtually any digital tool with ubiquitous broadband Internet access, which means just about anywhere there's a Starbucks or Panera, cellular coverage, or where we can aim a satellite antenna. We can easily work virtually. Millennial workers function well in virtual teams thanks to countless hours of on-line gaming, collaborating to solving complex problems with people they've never met in person.

This means we no longer care about the data center location because we can access it from everywhere. I.T. location becomes irrelevant, so let's put data centers where we can get the cheapest land and power.

Therefore, unless customers show up at a physical location to purchase goods or consume services, businesses don't need dedicated office space. You see this trend reflected in commercial office space and retail vacancy rates.

From Buying Efficiency to Buying Deployment Speed and Flexibility

In past decades, CIOs would architect and deploy I.T. systems with the vision of a five-year life span. With their best SWAG (scientific wild-ass guess) about future I.T. demands, they would architect a system overprovisioned and too expensive in the short run and under provisioned in the long run.

This has never been an efficient approach because data center purchases are the fastest declining assets in the business. Moore's Law predicts that they'd get the same equipment for 50 percent less in 12 to 18 months. Yet they still outfitted for a five-year lifespan.

Can you now imagine prepaying and locking yourself into a data center architecture for the next five years? That would be I.T. suicide.

Responsive Asset Deployment and Redeployment

We're rapidly making the transition from architecting for efficiency to orchestrating for flexibility.

Customers willingly pay more for flexibility when they consider the net present value of money and the agility of making rapid I.T. changes in response to chaotic business conditions and fickle customer demands.

> AN I.T. BUDGET THAT'S LAST YEAR'S NUMBER
> PLUS A PERCENTAGE INCREASE,
> INDICATES NO BUDGET-SETTING STRATEGY.

What's more, executives no longer tolerate the inefficiencies of traditional I.T. infrastructure management. The data center has operated under the auspices of a number of technology-centered tribes or clans, each curating a portion of the data center system with their own processes and politics, and each jealously defending their territory.

{ 33 }

For example, there's the server tribe, dominated the HPE Compaq tribe. There's the storage tribe, dominated by EMC. There's the network tribe, dominated by Cisco. There's the DBA tribe, dominated by Microsoft and Oracle, depending on company size. There's the power and cooling tribes, represented by different trade unions.

Any innovation requires cross-domain development, increasing complexity and adding more potential points of failure.

These tribes resist revision to their procedures because change unacceptably increases the probability of failure and downtime and the possibility of a career-ending event.

For executives to make any revisions to the I.T. infrastructure requires coercing all the tribes to sit around the campfire, pass the peace pipe, consider the mandated changes, and reluctantly agree. It takes time, persuasion, and horse trading.

> THE DATA CENTER'S RELUCTANCE AND RESISTANCE TO CHANGE IS THE SOLE REASON FOR ALL SHADOW I.T.

Is it any wonder that department heads from marketing and sales just pull out their corporate credit card and order up cloud-based web services instead of battling the tribes? As much as the data center might try, it won't stop.

Often executives view the data center as having the highest percentage of high-maintenance prima donnas in their operation. They'd cut them loose the moment they had a viable alternative.

You know it's true!

Predictably, this ultimately leads to eliminating on-staff data curators and the rise of business rules curators. The tribe functions get outsourced and someone becomes responsible for curating the business rules that manifest in I.T. orchestration.

I predict the CIO role pivoting to business rules curation in response to the business models set by the rest of the executive team.

From Pay-for-Ownership to Pay-for-Access

Most executives lived through the last decade of depression triggered by the economic crash of 2008/2009. They remember the layoffs, closing facilities, and losing good people that they couldn't afford to pay.

They no longer want to own their means of production, a business model that no longer makes sense in an outsourced, virtual digital age. They'd prefer to have a scalable infrastructure that grows and shrinks through business cycles.

Actually, they insist on it and so do their customers, constituents, and shareholders.

You can see how this aligns with other business model pivots and values realignment. It all makes sense.

From Technology Acumen to Data Acumen: Data-Defined Deployments

When you don't care about how you curate your data, I.T. acumen becomes less important and data acumen becomes king.

The I.T. team moves to understanding *data-defined deployments*, using business rules to decide where and how data gets processed, stored, and secured based on the immediate and future value of the data. In the process, I.T. becomes strategically driven instead of tactical. They become a profit center instead of a cost center.

DATA-DEFINED DEPLOYMENT
IS THE FUTURE OF I.T. ORCHESTRATION.

For example, high-velocity, time-sensitive data (such as customer transactions) gets priority, so it's quickly mined and served up to executive dashboards to make timely operational decisions. Lower velocity data (like emails) gets placed in the cloud because most workers access it from there anyway. Static, historic data gets relegated to a low-cost cloud provider offering cheap, low performance storage for occasional access and analysis.

> DECISION RISK OCCURS WHEN
> DATA NO LONGER REFLECTS CURRENT CONDITIONS
> BUT EXECUTIVES DON'T KNOW IT.

Data value declines over time, usually quite rapidly. The more time that passes between data collection and serving up data insights and foresight, the more that decision risk occurs because stale data doesn't always reflect current conditions.

There's Gold in that Old Data

In the past, after old data was mined for predicting financial outcomes, it became useless other than for meeting archive mandates, usually at the behest of government or lawyers who want a post mortem on a failed company to know who to sue.

Now, with AI and extensive data analysis capabilities, historic data can be mined for new insights and to train artificial intelligence how the world works. It's much like the new gold rush, where companies reprocess gold fields with new techniques, extracting value from where there once was none.

From Onsite I.T. to I.T. Everywhere

Instead of demanding use of only onsite[20] technology, companies choose the technology that best supports their business model no matter where the physical technology gets hosted.

The bottom line: valuable and meaningful I.T. exists everywhere. CIOs can no longer only take responsibility for the equipment to which the company holds title. They must curate data wherever it exists, whomever owns the hardware, however the transport, and whatever the access device. They desperately need help with this.

Want to help them?

Good! A few very simple business model pivots make this all work, and in the process, you'll make way more profit.

Ten Fundamental Business Rules Pivots

Making the pivot means you're going to change your business rules. In the rest of this book, we'll explore what is required to make the transition from Managed Services Provider to Business Services Provider.

Consider these following ten fundamental business rules you must put into place to make this transition work.

1. Stop Selling Products, Start Selling Outcome

When you focus on the product, your customer always compares you with other options, which makes you a commodity, invites price comparisons, and drives demands for discounts.

---

[20] I prefer the word *onsite* to *on premises*. Please don't ever use *on premise* because *premise* means "the basis for a position or argument" and so it confuses the executives.

> A CUSTOMER DOESN'T BUY I.T.,
> THEY BUY FUTURE REVENUE AND PROFITS
> OR AN ACCOMPLISHED MISSION.

When you focus on selling outcome (what the customer wants to achieve and avoid), price becomes less important because the customer is sold on the value of *what* you deliver instead of *how* you deliver it. Obviously, customers still must have confidence in your ability to deliver the outcomes you promise. More about this on page 76.

2. Deliver Systems Instead of Products

More customers want done-for-you experiences. With more time pressure and a shortage of good help, your customers want to buy everything ready assembled, getting the full package instead of just the pieces that they have to put together.

Systems and solutions create substantial increases in margins, especially when customers don't know how to price out the parts. More about this on page 45.

3. Bring New Products to Your Customers, Not New Customers to Your Products

While this business rule seems counterintuitive to some salespeople, experienced business people know that you always make more margin on subsequent sales than you do on the first sale.

Your most profitable business comes from customers who know, like, and trust you. You don't have to discount or use expensive sales tactics to get them to buy. They know you're a low risk, sure thing.

> "MORE MARGIN IS MADE ON THE SECOND SALE THAN ON THE FIRST."
> – JOEL BLOCK

While it's important to expand your customer base, it requires an investment in marketing and sales activities to do so. Make more margin now from your customers and reinvest that in prospecting for new ones.

4. Sell What You Value and Value What You Sell

It's hard to make solid margins on products and services that you don't like, value, or respect. If you feel you're overcharging for a product, it's almost impossible for you to sell at full price. So, either recognize the value of what you're selling and clearly articulate it in words your customers understand, or sell something you find valuable.

> LOWEST PRICE MOTIVATES ABOUT 15 PERCENT OF THE POPULATION AND THE FEDERAL GOVERNMENT.

Make sure you have a solid feeling of your value so that when you quote the price, your confidence makes the price stick.

5. Every Deal is Profitable, Strategic, or Both

A great way to make more margin is to say "no" to unprofitable deals.

> THE BEST WAY TO DRIVE YOUR COMPETITION OUT OF BUSINESS IS LET THEM HAVE ALL THE UNPROFITABLE BUSINESS.

You might be thinking, "Wait a second, Mark! I've worked hard to sell them and I'm going to close that deal even if I just break even on it."

Why? You think they'll place the next order at full price? Fuggetaboutit!

The only time you might consider no-margin deals is if it's a proof of concept and you have a contract for future business at margins that make business sense. Still, the problem with that is you've tipped your hand on how low you'll go, not the best position for the long haul. More about this on page 53.

6. Don't Close Deals, Open Relationships

Very few companies can be wildly successful with a business that relies on transactions.

Wouldn't you love it if on the first of the month you have sufficient sales to cover your expenses? That's what a relationship-based, recurring revenue business does for you.

> **A CUSTOMER CAN'T BUY UNTIL THEY TRUST YOU...**
> **TO DELIVER, TO CREATE VALUE, TO TELL THE TRUTH.**

To do this, shift your focus to opening relationships, not just closing deals.

7. Become a Trusted Business Partner Instead of a Trusted Technology Advisor

Many sales and business consultants recommend becoming a trusted advisor. While this seems a reasonable approach, an advisor is usually limited to a specific topic or technology, putting you in a box.

> **THE DESIRABLE DIFFERENCE BETWEEN YOUR PRODUCT**
> **AND ANOTHER OPTION IS OFTEN YOU.**

What's preferable: be positioned as a business advisor, providing insights, services, and products that support their business roadmap. Do this and you become a trusted partner, invited to the table anytime the company needs to figure out a way to implement their roadmap. From this position, you make substantially more margin. More about this on page 129.

8. Know What Motivates Every Buyer, Especially Executives

Old-school salespeople pitch features, advantages, and benefits trying to map the product to the customer's motivation, attempting to persuade and convince them to buy. The pitch ends with a today-only special price. It's hard work, creates a lot of friction, objections, and resistance along the way, and always erodes margins. And, it doesn't work anymore.

Instead, invest time to learn about your customers and what motivates them. When you map their motivation to the product instead of the other way around, sales becomes frictionless and you keep much more margin.

> WHAT MOTIVATES BUYERS IS OFTEN DIFFERENT THAN YOU THINK
> BECAUSE THEIR SUCCESS IS MEASURED DIFFERENTLY FROM YOURS.

Understand what motivates executives, the people that set budgets and approve major purchases. With this insight, you can do a much better job creating confidence that you are the best vendor, even when your prices may be higher than the competition. More about this on page 63.

9. Sell to Those Whose Job Depends on It

If you're talking to somebody who doesn't understand the value of what you're selling, they always ask for a discount, because any idiot can say, "That's too expensive!"

> STOP SELLING TO THOSE WHO CAN SAY "NO" BUT CAN'T SAY "YES."
> IT FRUSTRATES YOU BOTH.

Instead, sell to people who must have your offering to accomplish their job. Sell to people who give a damn about what you sell; they have appreciation, respect, understand the value, and can pay more when it makes their life easier, more efficient, and more flexible.

While your customers have a fiduciary responsibility to negotiate prices, this approach can reduce the number of times you go through the purchasing department meat grinder. Your business acumen and alignment with the executive's desired outcomes becomes the key competitive differentiator. More about this on page 45.

10. Understand Your Buyer's Negotiating Strategies and Have Counter Strategies Ready

Assume everyone who buys from you is a trained negotiator. Have you been trained to counter their tactics? If not, it's costing you margin in every deal you negotiate.

> A COMMERCIAL BUYER NEGOTIATING A LOWER PRICE IS TAKING MONEY OUT OF YOUR POCKET, BUT NOT PUTTING IT IN THEIRS.

Consider this: if you can negotiate fewer discounts to keep more margin, it's the same effect as raising your prices, driving more profits straight to the bottom line. You could pay for negotiation skills training with the increased margin of your next deal.[21] More about this on page 151.

---

[21] I co-authored *Guerrilla Negotiating* on how to counter buyer's dirty negotiating tricks and tactics. http://amzn.to/2igAmom

Get Ready to Pivot Your Business

Are you ready to start your journey from MSP to BSP? Are you feeling a bit of apprehension? Does it feel like someone's holding a gun to your head or like you're getting ready for a rollercoaster ride?

If it's like a gun to your head, you may want to sell your business and do something else.

If it feels exciting like a rollercoaster ride, let's go!

Chapter Summary

❑ Business models pivot from transactional revenue to recurring revenue.

❑ The business models and associated business rules of all players in the I.T. value chain undergo massive disruption and pivots.

❑ Traditional I.T. architecture and value propositions of efficiency don't support the new business models.

❑ I.T. moves from technology acumen to data acumen resulting in data-driven deployment.

❑ You'll need to intentionally change your business rules to deploy your business model shifts.

Ask Yourself

❑ What do I see happening in the business models of my customers?

❑ Do I want to help my customers with their business model pivots?

❑ Can I embrace the move to data-driven deployments, becoming a business services provider?

❑ Am I willing to learn what it takes to support the business model pivots of my vendors, my distributors, my customers, and my team?

❑ What business rules do I need to change?

Ask Your Team

❑ What changes do you foresee in customer business model pivots?

❑ Why do you think they're changing so rapidly?

❑ What do we need to do to stay ahead of our customer's value demands?

❑ What do we do when there's not much on-site hardware to manage?

Action Plan

❑ Talk with customer executives about their changing business models, specifically moving to recurring revenues and scalable systems.

❑ Identify the business rules you'll need to change to implement your new business model. These rules will change over time as you refine your business model.

❑ Have conversations about these four business model pivots to prove to yourself that they are real, impending, and inevitable.

❑ Share this chapter with trusted CIO customers to get their take on the future. You might save their career.

Chapter 4:
Pivot Factor –
From Efficiency to Flexibility

Traditional I.T. models focused on efficiency: creating systems, processes, and procedures that trimmed away the extra labor, costs, and waste by creating a uniform I.T. product at the lowest possible cost. This works well when there aren't many changes in technology, demand, and consumer expectation.

> THE TRADITIONAL BUSINESS MANTRA:
> "OWN THE MEANS OF PRODUCTION"
> NOW BECOMES A BUSINESS LIABILITY.

Traditional factories were designed and built over years to deliver goods that would be in the market for decades. Those market slots are full and being disrupted at every turn.

I'm seeing well-run companies stumbling because they can't move fast enough to keep up with the demands of their nimble – and fickle – customers. Think about how Dollar Shave Club wounded Gillette, now scrambling to catch up.

Traditional business models create a static system with so much inertia that meaningful change becomes a challenge. People involved don't want to change, management sees change as risky to their career, and change creates costs and inefficiencies counter to the business model. And they have plenty of evidence to support their position.

Yet, in today's rapidly moving world, the merely efficient get left behind. Businesses are closing at an unprecedented rate (mostly because of debt overload) despite all-time record highs on Wall Street. If you're stuck in your processes, you're at risk of being disrupted, and you won't detect it until it's too late.[22]

> ### "THAT'S HOW WE'VE ALWAYS DONE IT"
> ### INDICATES A FEAR OF FACING THE TRUTH.

What has to change?

The Pivot Towards Flexibility

Choosing a business model that embraces ever-changing technology and market demands requires corporate-wide flexibility and a willingness to forgo certainty for uncertainty. Even massive companies must be able to pivot in months if not weeks. The day of an 18-month I.T. project is coming to an end. It's replaced with rapid phased, scalable deployments: think lean and agile management methods on steroids.

From CapEx to OpEx

Capital funding strategies shift from long-term purchase and leases to short-term renting and subscription models. Customers can't pivot fast when the business model is based on long-term amortization of capital equipment and facilities. For this reason, they've got to transition from a capital expense (CapEx) based model to an operating expense (OpEx) business model. Expect tax code changes to become friendlier to short amortization schedules for rapidly advancing technology.

Transforming Through the Execution Risk

The biggest issue with moving from efficiency to flexibility is execution risk: how can customers execute when they don't know what they'll be executing? This requires a new executive mindset, new tools, new reward structure, new business

---

[22] https://www.bloomberg.com/graphics/2017-retail-debt/

model, and specific people in place with unique attitudes and skills.

Culture Pivot

And it takes more than that. It takes a massive culture shift. See the transformation model below.

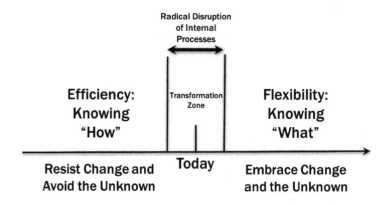

The Transformation from Efficiency to Flexibility

Making the transformation from efficiency as a key value to flexibility as a key value demands massive cultural disruption of internal processes, politics, and procedures. It's not for the faint of heart or the indecisive. Entering the transformation zone requires a complete overhaul of what's judged as right and wrong, what's good business and what's bad business. It's a complete reinvention of the organization and culture from the ground up.

At least one third of the existing companies won't make the transition, can't make the transition, and will make every excuse on the planet to avoid the transformation. And we'll see them on the scrap heap, in the bargain bin, and in MBA case studies.

Efficiency requires an expert understanding about the tactical *how* to accomplish a task or mission. The better you know how, the more efficient you become. There's much corporate resistance to change with a tendency to avoid the unknown because of the perceived risk to upsetting the processes and the perceived chaos that results.

> **"HOW CAN I MANAGE CHAOS?"**
> **"YOU DON'T. YOU SURF CHAOS."**

To be agile and flexible changes the focus to a strategic, *what* that has to be accomplished, knowing the tactical, *how* is a moving target. The faster you can identify the *what*, the sooner you'll be able to figure out – or outsource – the *how*. To do this, you and your team must embrace the unknown, considering every day to be an adventure and a battle to be won.

> **KNOWING HOW TO ACHIEVE YOUR VISION**
> **ALWAYS FOLLOWS CLARITY OF YOUR VISION.**
> **NEVER THE OTHER WAY AROUND.**

How to Navigate the Transformation

How can you make the transition to agility and flexibility? Consider these ideas.

Create a Culture of Speed

Stop the culture of "we need more data" and "let's decide next quarter." Instead, bring together the brightest new minds and put them into regular scrums so that you can "skate to where the puck's gonna be" to use a Wayne Gretsky metaphor. Take on the mindset of an entrepreneurial startup, willing and able to pivot as you get more intelligence.

Embrace Agile and Lean Methods

These methods allow rapid adjustment to processes, quickly correct issues, and can allow products to take flight fast. There are lots of great books on the topic, many excellent facilitators, and experienced team members ready to take it to a new level.

Expect Massive Fallout

In my experience, when you make massive transformation, one third of the team won't make it. It's too much for them to handle. The sooner you move them on, the smoother the transformation will be. If you don't, they'll actively sabotage the transition, and thoughtlessly take down the company. You probably know who they are. While they are good people providing valuable service in the past, they can't make the journey to the new world and now can tank the business. Let them go for the good of everyone else.

> CUT LOOSE THE NAYSAYERS TODAY.

One third will be on the fence. The sooner you can win them over, the better you'll be. Without a solid plan and swift execution, you'll lose half of them, which may terminate the transition.

And one third will be right on board. "It's about time! I thought I'd have to leave." These are your transformation champions. Round them up, give them the new direction, and get out of their way.

Turn Millennials Loose on the Problem

The good news: Millennials already know how to make rapid transformation based on their extensive experience playing video games. In that environment, they're not afraid to make mistakes knowing that they'll learn fast and take another shot at another approach.

While Boomers and some Gen X may resist this idea, the Millennials excel and will, by default, soon be running the world. If this freaks you out, you're in for a massive surprise because you're resisting the inevitable.

Adopt Lean Hierarchy Three-Level Leadership

Any time that an organization needs to successfully navigate change, they must embrace the concept of three level management and lean hierarchy.

Lean hierarchy, the foundation of effective organizational design, evaluates the current cognitive power at all levels of managerial leaders and matches them to the appropriate level of work complexity for maximum strategic, tactical, and task impact.

> "THE DOMINANT, MOST PROFITABLE PLAYER IN ANY MARKET IS OFTEN OPERATING AT ONE COGNITIVE LEVEL HIGHER THAN ITS COMPETITORS IN KEY COMPETITIVE FUNCTIONS." – ELLIOTT JAQUES

Three-level leadership, the cornerstone of strategy execution ensures that employees at every organizational level get two supporting and interacting managers:

1. A manager who is accountable for using fair and motivating managerial leadership practices with every direct report.
2. A mentor, the manager's manager, who ensures, through observation, that the manager is holding each direct report accountable for their work while adding value when needed.

This method rapidly installs new culture and processes in an organization that must change to succeed.[23]

Get Help

Get help from those who have paid the "stupid tax" on transformations like this. They know how.[24]

Chapter Summary

❑ A shift from efficiency, the driving factor of the age of manufacturing to flexibility, the driving factor of the age of digital disruption requires an overhaul of what we market, sell, and deliver.

❑ Generational shifts drive values and culture changes, challenging long held beliefs. Be willing to adjust.

❑ During the transition, be willing to discuss the visions and goals of executives. Leaders are out front with flexibility, laggards tenaciously cling to efficiency. They'll cost cut their way out of business.

Ask Yourself

❑ How can I pivot from efficient to flexible?

❑ What changes do I need to make in how I fund the capital expenses of my business? How do I pivot to an OpEx model?

❑ What do my business rules demand of my customers that limits my business potential?

❑ What old business truisms do I need to examine and release?

---

[23] Chris Stark is the master of this strategy. Talk with him. https://www.linkedin.com/pulse/lean-managerial-leadership-chris-stark/

[24] Join the community at MSPtoBSP.com

Ask Your Team

❏ What do you value more, efficiency or flexibility?

❏ What's driving the shift from paying for ownership to paying for access?

❏ What do we need to do to stay ahead of our customer's changing demands?

Action Plan

❏ Talk with customer executives about shifting views from efficiency to flexibility.

❏ Look for ways to bring flexibility to your business rules and processes.

❏ Identify where customers are willing to pay more for efficiency.

❏ Understand that not all customers will pay for flexibility, so sell them efficiency until they make the transition or cease operations.

Chapter 5:
Pivot Factor –
Serve the Entire
Data Value Hierarchy

Your most drastic business model pivot comes by expanding your business relationship from just the data center to a relationship with everybody whose livelihood depends on I.T.

Does that scare you a bit?

Good! That means we're moving out of your comfort zone – that place where you'll be disrupted and disbanded – into a paradigm where you're profitable and make a profound difference.

But, I Can't Go Over the CIO's Head

Many MSPs tell me that they can't go around the CIO to other executives out of fear of damaging the relationship. They may have been explicitly prohibited from doing so.

YOUR CIO RELATIONSHIPS WON'T MATTER
WHEN THEY'RE GONE.

Get over it! Remember, 80 percent of data centers will go away. On page 147 you'll learn why CIOs are so resistant to you speaking with their executives and how to expand your relationships and do no harm. In fact, you'll move your relationship with the CIO to a whole new level of improved respect.

CUSTOMERS DO BUSINESS WITH PEOPLE
WHO THEY KNOW, LIKE, AND TRUST...
AND THANKS TO SOCIAL MEDIA, WHO LIKE THEM BACK.

Let's consider who else you need to know, and who needs to know, like, and trust you to grow your business and radically improve profits.

The Data Value Hierarchy

There are three fundamental roles when dealing with data: curators, creators, and consumers. At each level, the value of the data increases by at least an order of magnitude with commensurate increase in supporting budgets, money you're probably not accessing. Yet!

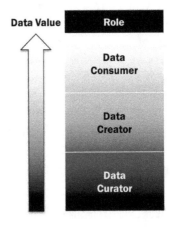

The Data Value Hierarchy:
Data Value Increases as it Moves Up the Hierarchy
from Curators to Creators to Consumers

Let's dig into each of these levels.

Data Curators

Data curators live in the data center, concerned about data security, system manageability, data compatibility across databases, and data availability – keeping the bad guys out and not making it too difficult for the good guys to access data when and where they want. Their job is to maintain the data systems and manage the data.

Do the data curators care about the data?

DATA CURATORS SEE NO VALUE IN THE DATA.

No! They couldn't care less about the data. They don't care if it's candid pictures of cats or the cure for cancer, it's all the same to them. They care about the data integrity, but care not about the data itself.

As long as the data they are tasked to oversee is secure and available, so is their job and career. But if the system goes down or there's a compromise, their career is on the line. If the issue isn't resolved and cleaned up quickly, their career options default to The Geek Squad or selling I.T.

You're laughing because it's true.

Yet, most of the recent advances in I.T. (big data, flash storage, mobile devices, XaaS, etc.) go way beyond the data curation realm, providing new business value. The vast majority of these value propositions become lost on the I.T. department.

These innovations become more of a threat than a benefit to CIOs because of potential operational disruption and system downtime triggered by new, unknown technology.

SHADOW I.T. EXISTS WHEN
THE NEEDS OF THE COMPANY CHANGE FASTER
THAN THE ABILITY OF THE CIO TO RESPOND.

Typically, data curation only extends to the systems that the data center owns or leases. Anything that the CIO doesn't specify, fund, or control they disparagingly call *shadow I.T.,* *rogue I.T.,* or *stealth I.T.*

Traditionally, MSPs and VARs sell to the data-curating I.T. team and rarely have a relationship with any executive other than the CIO.

Digital disruption negatively impacts the data curation team because of their inability to keep up and figure out how to manage rapid change and new technologies. These are the people being displaced by I.T. disruption.

Face it, your traditional customer contacts are fading away.

What Data Curators Want: Visibility to Manage

Data curators want to feel safe and want to be able to *manage* the data to bring more value to the curation system that they've architected.

Data Value	Role	Requirements	Result
	Data Consumer		
	Data Creator		
	Data Curator	Security Manageability Compatibility	Visibility Flexibility Job Security

Data Value Hierarchy – Data Curator Strategy:
Visibility into the I.T. Ecosystem to Manage Data Anywhere

Data Curator Business Risk

The new key to solid uptime SLAs in mixed systems: *visibility* into the operations of the entire I.T. ecosystem.

When an end user doesn't get the data they want, when they want, as fast as they want it, they blame I.T. even when the problem is caused by their personal mobile device or an app they just downloaded.

Without ecosystem visibility, the curator ends up with unexpected performance problems and unexplained downtime, expensive troubleshooting, and ultimately job loss. No wonder they won't touch shadow I.T.

Visibility brings *flexibility* because the curator can manage the data no matter where it exists. Ultimately this combination brings *job security* to a career that's under attack.

Your BSP pivot brings visibility to every aspect of the business system, no matter the location or ownership of the compute power, storage, applications, or user device.

You do this with complete system virtualization (VM, SDN, data fabrics[25], security fabrics, cloud, etc.), orchestration tools, disaster recovery and business continuity strategies, back up XaaS vendors, and overarching data protection systems.

Data Creators

Data creators are all the people who collect and generate data as part of their job.

In corporations, finance, sales, marketing, R&D, and manufacturing all generate mission critical data.

In government, these people collect census data, economic information, and intelligence.

These are also the people who make movies, design games, and record music for consumers.

When creators can't generate data, they're not working.

Do they care about how their data is curated?

No! They couldn't care less.

---

[25] A data fabric knits together data infrastructure including device, cloud, disk, flash, and cache for access management and performance optimization so that applications and users automatically get the right storage resources at the right time.

When I.T. drags their feet, there's a direct impact on the creator's efficiency, effectiveness, and their career.

> **DATA CREATORS DON'T CARE HOW THEIR WORK GETS CURATED,
> JUST THAT THEY CAN WORK FAST
> AND THAT IT WON'T GET LOST.**

Data creators willingly buy XaaS if necessary to make work possible, easy, and faster. This is why business tools providers like Intuit's QuickBooks, Salesforce.com, and HubSpot.com have grown to be massive companies.

What Data Creators Want

Data creators demand easy *accessibility* to data and *collaboration* systems, and choose specialized tools to perform their work with *efficiency*. The result is increased *productivity* and *innovation*. When frustrated, they leave, so *job satisfaction* is key to retaining the best data creators.

Data Value	Role	Requirements	Result
	Data Consumer		
	Data Creator	Accessibility Collaboration Efficiency	Productivity Innovation Job Satisfaction
	Data Curator		

Data Value Hierarchy – Data Creator Strategy:
Create Data as Efficiently and Innovatively as Possible

The data creators have a pretty good idea about data growth expectations and future requirements that the data curators don't have. When you're designing customer infrastructure, ignoring the creators means you'll underestimate future capacity demand.

Data Creator Business Risk

Data creators often don't consider data protection and business continuity issues. They probably aren't aware of security policy implications and implementations. They may not recognize the business risk of data leakage or compromise. If their favorite XaaS vendor goes down in flames, they're toast.

They probably need assistance with data integration and API connectors to other tools and internal systems.

They need your help!

Here's the good news: most XaaS vendors rely on your support and services for your shared customers. They can't grow their business without you. You'll probably find them more willing to engage and support you than traditional I.T. vendors who are busy servicing bigger clients.

Data Consumers

Data consumers – at the top of the data value hierarchy – rely on data to make executive decisions, formulate battlefield orders, or in the case of consumers, to be entertained or educated. At this level, data becomes mission critical. Easy, secure access to the freshest data becomes a competitive advantage.

Data consumers decide how to spend money to get the data they demand. They are the source of all I.T. (or consumer technology) budgets and they'll invest what they need to accomplish their mission, whether corporate or personal.

What Data Consumers Want

Data consumers expect data to be *reliable, predictable,* and *secure* so that they can have *accurate foresight* to direct resources to monetize their data for *profitability* or *mission accomplished*. Or, just be entertained or educated.

Data Value	Role	Requirements	Result
	Data Consumer	Reliability Predictability Security	Accurate Foresight Mission Accomplished Profitability
	Data Creator		
	Data Curator		

Data Value Hierarchy – Data Creator Strategy:
Gain Accurate Foresight to Profitably Monetize Data or Accomplish Their Mission

Data Consumer Business Risk

When data consumers believe that data is accurate, timely, and relevant, they'll make decisions based on reports filtered through their experience, intuition, business model, and objectives. Stale data, inaccurate data, or false data has serious impact on their performance. You get to help them design and implement data-quality systems to ensure against this issue.

For data consumers, data velocity becomes important and decision risk becomes real. Most of the innovations in I.T. target data consumers, such as flash storage providing substantially faster access to data and speeds data mining operations. If you're not having conversations at this level, your flash value propositions fall on deaf ears.

Chapter Summary

❏ Your primary business pivot: sell to the entire data value hierarchy, each with a different objective and strategy.

Data Value	Role	Requirements	Result
⬆	Data Consumer	Reliability Predictability Security	Accurate Foresight Mission Accomplished Profitability
	Data Creator	Accessibility Collaboration Efficiency	Productivity Innovation Job Satisfaction
	Data Curator	Security Manageability Compatibility	Visibility Flexibility Job Security

❏ The value of data increases dramatically as you go up the hierarchy with the most value at the top. They set budgets and objectives for I.T. to implement.

❏ Key I.T. value propositions appeal to data consumers and data creators, not data curators.

❏ Sell to the values and key performance indicators of each layer of the hierarchy to be relevant and valuable.

❏ The top two levels don't care about how their data is curated, so you won't have technical conversations with them. Instead you'll have business discussions.

Ask Yourself

❏ What do I need to do to pivot my business to bring value to the entire data value hierarchy?

❏ Can I call above or around the CIO of my clients? If not, can I get over my reluctance?

❏ Who do I need to engage with to trigger conversations with the top of the data value hierarchy?

❑ How do I change my conversations to be relevant and valuable to the upper levels of the hierarchy?

❑ How do I pivot my marketing and sales to engage with these more profitable and lower resistance players?

Ask Your Team

❑ We need to engage with data creators and data consumers. Are you willing to learn how to do this?

❑ What types of shadow I.T are our clients buying? Can we support this technology?

❑ What do our customer data creators and consumers need to improve their operations?

❑ How can we tap into those budgets for our business?

Action Plan

❑ Expand your thinking to involve all levels of the data value hierarchy.

❑ Start conversations with the data consumers you know about their business vision to get experience in talking with them.

❑ Catalog the shadow I.T. that your customers use now to identify vendors that you're willing to support.

Chapter 6:
Pivot Factor –
Sell to Prospect Motivation

Introductory note: the discussion about prospect motivation is in the context of business-to-business (B2B) sales of I.T.: selling high-consideration, long-sales cycle, team decision-based, mission critical products and services. (More about this on page 151.) Commodity and business-to-consumer (B2C) sales situations use a different selling mode, yet there are similarities.[26]

Your Business Success Factors

What's the secret to guaranteeing business success? Is it a great product? Killer marketing? The perfect sales pitch? Nope, those are only ten percent of your success and if you focus on that, you're missing massive opportunity.

> ONLY 10 PERCENT OF YOUR SALES SUCCESS
> DEPENDS ON THE PRODUCT.

Many companies believe that a great product will sell itself. They think that when they create a bunch of unique value propositions and present them like a flower bouquet, prospects will immediately see the value and enthusiastically buy. They're convinced that if the sales team has a persuasive and compelling presentation that prospects will sign on the spot.

Not true, especially for high-consideration products and services. Salespeople have this belief that they can and must

---

[26] For a broader discussion of effective sales modes, read my book, *Selling Disruption*. http://SellingDisruption.com

persuade a new prospect to "sell" them on the first contact. They forget that the basis of all sales is trust, more so than ever.

I point the blame to historically bad sales culture, poor sales management, old-school sales trainers, and Hollywood's portrayal of "Sell me this pen." You reject those sales methods and so do your prospects.

The biggest business mistake is using low consideration sales tactics – that is initially putting attention on your product instead of the outcome prospects want – in high consideration sales situations. Why do we do this?

The Origin of Traditional Sales Methods

Many salespeople rely on techniques developed more than a century ago. In the 1887, John Henry Patterson, founder of National Cash Register (NCR)[27] founded the first sales school based on a prepared sales presentation, requiring the sales team to memorize road-tested scripts, master a "book of arguments" to counter objections, and practice proven closing statements.

It was so effective that it became the Holy Grail of sales with today's common sales methods based on that original 16-page manual.[28]

> "AFTER YOU HAVE MADE YOUR PROPOSITION CLEAR AND FEEL SURE THAT THE MERCHANT REALIZES THE VALUE OF THE REGISTER, DO NOT ASK FOR AN ORDER, TAKE FOR GRANTED THAT HE WILL BUY."
> – NCR SALES PRIMER, 1887

---

[27] https://en.wikipedia.org/wiki/John_Henry_Patterson_(NCR_owner)

[28] http://hbswk.hbs.edu/item/john-h-patterson-and-the-sales-strategy-of-the-national-cash-register-company-1884-to-1922

An estimated one-sixth of the top executives in the nation's companies from 1910 to 1930 were NCR-trained sales professionals.[29] (Patterson was quite a character, known for terminating employees by publicly burning their desk on the factory lawn, introducing forever into our language, "You're fired!")[30]

Old school selling claims that a good salesperson can sell anything to anyone. That may have been true to a slick snake oil salesman conning a country bumpkin in the last Century.

Times have changed. Your prospects are intelligent, educated, jaded, and suspicious; with the old sales model, you can barely sell them a product they know, like, and trust.

Today's buyers hate and reject this approach. You resist it. What makes you think it works with your savvy prospects? In fact, you might feel guilty, blaming yourself for why those broken methods aren't working. Stop it!

The Difference Between Decision and Commitment

Modern sales is about intelligent conversations, which facilitate a transaction that a prospect has already decided to make, in your case, changes in the business rules that underlie their pivoting business model. Sales activity occurs between when a prospect decides to make a change and when they make the commitment to buy.

What's the difference between deciding and committing?

Have you *decided* to go on vacation this year? If not, stop reading and make plans; you need to get a life.

Have you *committed* to go on vacation this year?

What's the difference? Tickets!

The difference between decision and commitment is the transaction. The time between when your prospect has made a

---

[29] http://articles.chicagotribune.com/2001-04-22/news/0104220276_1_register-agents-restored

[30] http://www.dayton.com/lifestyles/things-you-didn-know-about-ncr-john-patterson/K65i9ONHk46rKchxEUN2BN/

decision but hasn't made the commitment is when your sales activities have impact.

Marketing, Sales, and Service Roles
in a Prospect's Journey to Decision and Commitment.

When a prospect engages with you, they've made a decision to make a purchase, and they're acting on that decision – performing research, getting pricing, choosing a vendor, making the transaction. Their priorities determine how fast this goes.

If it's an urgent problem, they'll buy as soon as you can prove that you can solve their problem. If it's less urgent, it will take time until the prospect's priorities shift to make the commitment.

When calling prospects, you're looking for people who have decided but not yet made a commitment. All other conversations aren't sales, but prospecting or marketing activities, informing potential prospects about something they didn't yet know you could do, or customer service, maintaining the relationship so that you're on their short list when they next decide.

How do you uncover where they are in their purchase process? Ask questions like these:

"What are your plans around ..."

"What's on your shopping list for…"

"What's on your wish list for…"

Their answer tells you what information they need, what offers they'd find attractive, and their purchase priority.

Why Buyers are Liars

You might be thinking, "But, Mark that's not how sales works. I have lots of interested prospects that I can sell to."

Oh, yah? Why haven't you closed them?

I'll tell you why.

People invent lies about you to justify their rude behavior towards your sales activities. That's why bad cold calling degrades your brand – they hang up on you and make up a reason for doing so that puts you in a negative light. Cold-called prospects become more averse to doing business with you then if you had never called them. If you were around in the 1980s, you probably remember those discount long distance service cold calls during dinnertime? Didn't do much for the MCI brand, did it.

Prospects often position their decision as "I'm thinking about…" because they know that if they tell a salesperson, "I've decided to buy…" they will be a target for high pressure sales tactics. For this reason, prospects act less interested than they are. Conversely, prospects will act more interested if they want something that you're offering, such as a giveaway.

> PROSPECTS WILL TELL YOU
> WHAT THEY THINK YOU WANT TO HEAR
> TO GET YOU TO DO WHAT THEY WANT.

You may want to read the above line again. There's powerful understanding in those words.

The solution to this? Take the spotlight off the product and place it on the outcome that your prospect seeks. Instead of pitching your product, understand what your prospect wants to experience. This switch in attention subtly, yet profoundly changes the dynamic between sales professional and prospect, to the benefit of both. Let's explore this further.

The Marketing and Sales Success Formula

Three factors determine successfully selling to a prospect: 50 percent of your success is based on your prospect's motivation, 40 percent is based on your relationship, and 10 percent is based on the product or service that you're selling.[31]

Selling Success Factors

What Happens When There's No Motivation

Half of your success is based on prospect motivation. Do they want what your product does? Do they have the capacity to consider it right now? Do they find it valuable, relevant, and meaningful? It matters not how good your offer, how great your price, how incredible the deal, if your prospect isn't motivated, they'll refuse even if you offer to give it to them.

Have you ever experienced the situation where you gave your prospect a trial loaner, and when you came back later, they hadn't touched it? No motivation.

---

[31] This model is adapted from the work of Bruce Joyce about adult learning, which is the essence of selling and change management.

> "TO ACT IS TO BE COMMITTED,
> AND TO BE COMMITTED IS TO BE IN DANGER."
> – JAMES BALDWIN

Here's the problem with this tactic: buyers will invent a reason for not paying attention to your product. And their reason isn't good for your position, your brand, or your opportunity for future sales.

Only proceed with sales activity when you understand your prospect's motivation or you run the risk of making things worse.

Relationship Powers Sales

The relationship with your prospect determines if your product is a safe decision. Does your prospect trust you? Do they believe you? Do they feel that you're acting in their best interest? Or are you just trying to manipulate them into buying something that you're spiffed on this week?

> A PROSPECT BUYS WHEN THEY BECOME CONFIDENT
> ABOUT CHOOSING YOU.

A prospect becomes a customer when they feel *confident* that you can be trusted, that your product will deliver their desired outcome, and that if there are problems, you'll fix them.

It doesn't matter how motivated the prospect, if they don't trust you, they'll choose another, safer place to purchase, except in a dire emergency.

> A TRUSTING PROSPECT RELATIONSHIP IS THE PRICE
> OF EARNING THE RIGHT TO SELL TO THEM.

Your initial goal is to initiate a relationship that becomes the basis for their confidence. All sales success follows from this.

Product Positioning When the Time's Right

Surprised that product is only 10 percent of your success? You shouldn't be. All of your competitors do a good enough job or no one would buy from them and risk their career. To bash your competition is to insult all of those customers who consciously chose them; don't call your prospects stupid. Normal psychology states that a person tends to make the best choice based on the information available when they choose. When they selected a competitive product, it was the best choice in that moment.

> INSTEAD OF ASKING, "HOW CAN I BEAT MY COMPETITION?" ASK "HOW CAN I HELP MY CUSTOMERS BEAT THEIR COMPETITION?"

Most salespeople put all of their attention on the product during a prospect conversation.

Big mistake!

That's like going to a doctor's office and the doctor greets you with prescription pad in hand, writing out a drug order.

"Here's what you need" she says, tearing off the 'script.

"Wait a minute, Doc. You don't even know what's wrong with me."

"Sure I do! You're middle age. I know exactly what you need."

"What? What are you talking about?"

"Statins. No doubt you have high cholesterol. Besides, that's what I'm spiffed on this week."

You're laughing because it's true.

"In sales, as in medicine, prescription before diagnosis is malpractice," as *Acorn Principle* author, Jim Cathcart likes to say.

Leading with your product creates sales resistance and makes your job so much more challenging.

THE SECRET TO SALES: LEAD WITH THE PROSPECT'S NEED.

When you call a prospect and say, "I want to come see you about our amazing, incredibly priced product that will change your life!" they respond with, "No!" You're using an 1870's sales approaches with a sophisticated buyer. No wonder you're struggling.

The Heart of Selling is the 90 Percent

The heart of selling is the 90 percent sum of motivation and relationship. When you can create a trusted relationship and understand your prospect's motivation, you can sell them anything that accomplishes their desired outcome.

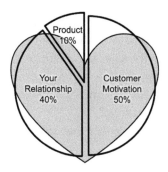

The Heart of Selling is the 90 Percent Combination of Relationship Plus Motivation

To illustrate this, you've no doubt successfully sold products that compete with the products you now sell. And you'll probably successfully sell competing products in the future. It's not the product that makes your success, it's your mastery of the 90 percent motivation and relationship. The real competitive is difference is you!

One more proof point: think back to the last time you had a sales challenge. What was the problem? Was it prospect motivation, your relationship, or the product? I'll bet it was an unmotivated prospect or you didn't understand their motivation clearly.

See how you can use this model to troubleshoot sales problems?

Features, Advantages, and Benefits. Oh My!

In the old sales model, you'd talk about a product's *features*, which create customer *advantages*, that translate to customer *benefits*. You recognize this.

When I worked for HP back in the mid 1980's, I'd create FAB charts (Features, Advantages, and Benefits) that would clearly show my product was the winner. Yet when I studied the competitor's FAB sheets, they ended up on top. Clearly, FAB is subjective.

FAB-based selling attempts to map the product to the prospect's motivation. Hopefully, the more compelling the FAB, the more persuasive the sales argument. Yes, in the 1870s, it was called a sales *argument*.

Wait a moment, this assumes you want to argue with your prospects. Sound persuasive?

It's not. It creates resistance that kills deal momentum.

> MAKING A CANNED PRESENTATION WITHOUT FIRST UNDERSTANDING YOUR PROSPECT'S MOTIVATION IS SALES SUICIDE.

The Biggest Problem with FAB-based Sales

Here's the problem: when you assert a value statement that the prospect doesn't find relevant, they *object*.

> UNTIL A SALESPERSON SPEAKS,
> THERE ARE NO OBJECTIONS,
> ONLY UNMET WANTS.

Face it, every objection that you've ever had to overcome came from you: you made a claim that your prospect found objectionable. Canned sales pitches are the source of all objections.

There's a clinical term for this: stupid!

I've found that if you create three or more objections during your sales pitch, that it's impossible to overcome them to win the deal.

When you have multiple decision makers involved in the conversation, the odds of presenting the perfect pitch that won't raise objections is close to zero because each person has a different opinion of value and risk. What one person finds useful, another finds objectionable. A FAB-based pitch to a decision team in the absence of research causes delays for complex sales because it often creates more problems than it solves.

Eliminate Objections Forever

What's the fix for this? Don't talk FAB until you know what motivates each prospect on the decision-making team. Declaring value before understanding objectives is like the doctor writing the prescription before knowing what you need: it kills trust and prevents a relationship.

Map FAB to Motivation

There is an exception to the rule: if the product is low-consideration, low risk, low cost, and can be bought with a few minutes of prospect consideration, FAB selling is efficient. It's how consumer packaged goods (CPG) get sold: create a customer avatar, identify their motivation, create FAB that trigger those motivations. This is classic Four Ps of marketing: Product, Position, Placement, Price.

You typically don't need a salesperson for that simple transaction. Your value is in facilitating bigger deals and higher-consideration purchases.

Stop Selling Only Pain

You've probably been taught to identify prospect pains, make them really feel it, and offer a solution that makes the pain go away. This may work for low-consideration purchases for a single decision maker, but it fails miserably for high-consideration, multiple decision maker deals.

The lower in the organization, the more pain avoidance you'll find, along with risk avoidance, and the ability to say no, but not the ability to say yes.

The higher in the organization, the more you'll find thought leadership, future vision, and long-term planning. At this level, it's not pain avoidance, it's dream manifestation. Push on their pains and you're likely to learn that a good solution to their pain is throwing you out of their office.

It's not just about the pains that they want to eliminate. Along with understanding what they want to avoid, you must explore their dreams and desires. Your competitors may be able to get rid of a prospect's pains, but the prospect dream space is where you identify unstoppable competitive differentiation. Now, you're exploiting opportunities, not just solving problems.

Explore Frustrations

Instead of pain, a much better word to use is *frustration.* You'll find people are reluctant to discuss pain with a stranger because they own the pain, may feel inadequate because they are experiencing pain, and may take responsibility for the cause of the pain. A source of frustration is rarely their responsibility, so they are more likely to discuss frustrations with you.

What question would you rather answer? "What's your pain?" or "What's frustrating you?"

You get it.

What Changes?

It's time to reverse the traditional sales approach. Stop forcing a square peg into a round hole, start learning what peg will fit.

> INSTEAD OF TRYING TO MAP PRODUCT FEATURES TO PROSPECT MOTIVATION, MAP PROSPECT MOTIVATION TO PRODUCT OUTCOMES.

When you understand your prospect's motivation and then map that to the product, sales happen like magic. Doing this reduces resistance, eliminates objections, and speeds the deal.

Uncovering Prospect Motivation

How do you map your prospect's motivation? Ask smart questions. In this situation, the naturally curious sales professional wins.

> "I HAVE NO SPECIAL TALENTS. I AM ONLY PASSIONATELY CURIOUS."
> – ALBERT EINSTEIN

You need to understand three things before you have *any* detailed discussion about the product:

1. Their objectives (what they wish to accomplish and avoid),
2. Their priorities (the sequence in which they achieve their objectives), and

3. Their criteria (what they find valuable and how they'll decide who will help them).

You must discover them in this order or you'll create unnecessary resistance.

> YOUR PROPOSITIONS HAVE NO VALUE
> UNTIL THEY ALIGN WITH YOUR PROSPECT'S
> OBJECTIVES, PRIORITIES, AND CRITERIA.

When you talk about your products in the absence of prospect knowledge, you're shooting in the dark and likely to hit your foot.

Understanding Prospect Objectives

Objectives describe what they need to do and avoid, and the motivation for doing it. It defines their desired outcome. *What* (the objective) and *why* (the motivation) define *strategy*.

For every person involved in the decision, there is a unique set of objectives based on their role, responsibility, temperament, and key performance indicators, all influenced by their current emotional state.

Seems like a lot to keep track of. It may be, yet in general, the decision will ultimately rest on one to three top objectives.

For business-to-business prospects, objectives map to their key performance indicators (KPIs), the measurement that lets them keep their job. If their KPI is high, they stay. If it's low, they go, right now.

All executives buy to support their KPIs and refuse to buy anything that could undermine them. When discovering KPIs, also find out who's keeping score by paying attention to the indicators, because that is where the ultimate power lies.

> ### YOUR PROSPECT'S OBJECTIVES
> ### SUPPORT THEIR CAREER.
> ### HELP THEM ACHIEVE THOSE OBJECTIVES
> ### AND THEY'LL MAKE YOUR CAREER.

Uncover objectives with open ended questions like these:

❑ What do you need to accomplish? Why? (Identify key objectives.)

❑ What are you trying to avoid? Why? (Identify risk factors.)

❑ What will this be like when it meets your satisfaction? (Their vision of the desired state.)

❑ What does success look like for this project? (Their definition of success.)

❑ What's holding you back from accomplishing this? Is it people, money, infrastructure, intellectual property, data analysis, or politics? (These are the six main reasons why executives get frustrated.)

❑ What happens if you don't accomplish this objective? (Explores the cost of failure.)

The more general the question at this stage, the better you'll to understand their motivational map.

> ### "BUSINESSES DON'T HAVE PROBLEMS,
> ### THEY HAVE EXPENSES."
> ### - JOEL BLOCK

All business problems fall into the category of expenses. They can throw money at problems until they go away. Got a legal problem? It becomes a legal expense. Got a sales problem? It becomes of selling expense. Got a product problem? It becomes a product development expense. You want to be in a position to catch that money.

Objectives often include increasing efficiency, improving flexibility, risk management, and fostering innovation. Commercial executive objectives look to grow revenue and market share, reduce operating and sales costs, and improve cash flow.

Efficiency allows for more profits for a given level of sales and allows for growth without additional capital investment.

Flexibility permits navigating rapidly changing situations to take advantage of new situations and survive market disruption.

Risk management considers at how to mitigate, reduce, eliminate, and insure against risks that can impact the operation.

Innovation creates competitive advantage and the opportunity for more profits. Innovation usually focuses on refining business models, creating new products and services, and improving customer experiences.

Do you have any control over your prospect's objectives? No, not a bit. Their objectives are set by the boss. You better understand them and position your product to support their objectives or you'll have no hope of a deal.

Probing Prospect Priorities

Priorities define the order in which tasks get done. It's the *where* and *when* decision that defines the *sequence* of events.

Do you have a prospect who has said, "Let's do it!" but they haven't yet placed the order? This is a priority problem. Making the commitment of placing the order isn't a high enough priority.

Do you have any control over your prospect's priorities? Think so? When was the last time a salesperson rearranged your priorities? If they made the attempt, how did they do it? They offered you a better price or made the product feel like it was scarce and if you didn't act right now, you wouldn't get what you wanted.

If the product is truly scarce, that's a great tactic. If it's manufactured scarcity, you're skating on thin ice, acting out of integrity. If your prospect discovers that it's not really scarce, you blow your trust – the basis of all successful sales relationships.

If you're selling a high-consideration product, be careful using scarcity as a closing tactic because the products are customized and the prospect knows you'll make one just for them.

Priorities can be assessed on a number of dimensions. When determining priorities, use open-ended questions. Don't ask questions that start with "Do you...", "Are You...", "Have you...", "Will you...", as you don't get enough data to make a determination with just a yes or no answer.

Let's consider the four priority areas that drive most purchase decisions.

Budget

A set budget is a solid indicator of priority. If they have a budgetary number, they've made some consideration of cost or investment and therefore have made the initial decision to purchase. High-consideration purchases almost always have a budgeting phase and low-consideration purchases rarely do, instead being purchased out of an expense fund or operations budget.

Don't ask, "Do you have a budget?" Closed ended questions don't give you the information you need.

Ask "What's your budget?" and you'll get one of three answers:

1. We don't have one.
2. I'm not going to tell you.
3. It's _____.

If they don't have a budget, offer to help them construct one. "We're the people who help companies like yours plan and budget so there are no surprises." Lack of budget is always a priority problem.

> "WHEN PEOPLE SAY, 'I DON'T HAVE THE MONEY',
> IT'S FICTION. PEOPLE ALWAYS HAVE MONEY
> TO DO WHAT THEY WANT. BROKE PEOPLE MAKE BAIL."
> – JOEL BLOCK

If they won't tell you the budget, it's because it's either embarrassingly small or they've had an experience where a salesperson discovered their budget and forced them to spend all of it. In this case, they're protecting their number.

Ask, "What was last year's budget?" They'll usually tell you because the money is spent. Next ask, "Is this year's budget a percentage larger or smaller?" They'll probably tell you. "By how much?" Some will tell you and some won't. In either case, you know that there wasn't much thought put into the budget if it is an increment or decrement from the prior year. You'll need to educate them on how to budget.

If they give you the budget number, never make the rookie mistake of saying, "We can work with that!" Instead ask, "Under what circumstances could that increase?" You'll find out if there's opportunity to expand the budget and how to do it.

Ask exploratory smart questions (with the items in parentheses being the underlying information to understand):

❑ How did you determine the budget? (Did they do research, or is it a SWAG?)

❑ What does it include? (Identifies their level of need analysis.)

❑ What do you think it leaves out? (Opens conversation for a bigger budget.)

❑ What other departments might contribute to the budget? (Are there other budget sources?)

❑ Are you considering a subscription type of purchase? (Are they pivoting to the new business models?)

❑ How does the budget take into account options for leases or other financing? (Is financing part of the deal?)

❏ Under what circumstances could that budget increase?
(Other expansion opportunities?)
❏ What is budget deployment timing? (How do cash flows
impact budget distribution?)
❏ Who has to sign off on this purchase? (Who's the approv-
ing person?)
❏ What's it cost for things to remain as they are? (Identify the
costs of doing nothing.)
❏ What's it worth for you to proceed? (Identify the value of
moving forward.)

With these last two questions, you've established a defensible budgetary range. If you can solve the problem for less than
the cost of doing nothing and they can make more from proceeding than the proposed investment, you have a viable cost
model.

You can now calculate the cost of waiting. Present this to
the strategist and budget approver and you can potentially create new urgency and shift priorities to close the deal sooner.

Scorekeeper

Who sets the KPIs? Who's paying attention to this project and
keeping score? The higher up the food chain, the higher the
priority. If this is a board of directors driven initiative, it's high
priority. If it's a front-line worker, probably not so much. You
need to understand who is watching this project to make sure
you don't get surprised by a competitor who knows more
about the account than you do.

The more people paying attention, the more complex the
deal. In this situation, carefully map the purchase process to
manage the moving parts, allocate resources, and orchestrate
the players.

Ask smart questions to determine who's involved:
❏ Who's driving this initiative? (Identifies the project lead,
but not necessarily the ultimate decision maker.)

- ❑ Who has this as part of their management objectives? (Identifies KPI drivers.)
- ❑ Who decides how to measure the success of this project? (Identifies who's setting the KPIs)
- ❑ Who wants this to succeed? (Identifies potential allies.)
- ❑ Who wants things to remain as they are now? (Identifies potential resistance.)
- ❑ Who decides what needs to be done? (Identifies the strategist.)
- ❑ Who decides how to pay for it? (Identifies the financial commitment maker.)
- ❑ Who determines acceptable ROI? (Identifies financial overseer.)
- ❑ How do they determine ROI? (Either align with their metric or teach them additional metrics.)
- ❑ Who determines how it gets done? (Identifies the tactical person who will deploy.)
- ❑ Who ultimately is responsible for the success of this project? (Identifies the top responsible party.)
- ❑ If there's a problem, who's most likely to get upset? (Identifies those who must consider the risk.)
- ❑ Whose job depends on this? (Identifies end users and potential critics.)
- ❑ What is the process your team uses to purchase something like this? (Identify their process, if they have one.)
- ❑ Who makes the ultimate approval or refusal? (Identify the ultimate decision maker.)
- ❑ Who is involved in the approval cycle? (Maps the approval team.)
- ❑ What do they consider important? (Identify the team members' criteria.)
- ❑ What's the approval path look like? (Maps the buying process, which becomes your sales process.)
- ❑ Who has approved a purchase like this in the past? (Identify past decision power to understand preferences.)

❑ How will they be involved this time? (What is their impact this time, there may be politics involved.)

❑ How did they make the decision last time? (Uncover decision making process.)

This set of smart questions lets you map the players in the deal, those you need to engage with and identify their motivators when you're involved with complex, high-consideration purchases.

Commitments

Identify what promises and commitments have been made, what resources are allocated, and what's been done so far. The more commitments, the higher the priority and the less likely the project will be cancelled. Ask smart questions like these:

❑ Who has made promises based on the completion of this project? (Whose job is on the line?)

❑ Who is responsible for the success of this project? (Whose career advancement is on the line?)

❑ Who is staking their career on this? (Who has the biggest motivation for a positive outcome?)

❑ What resources have you allocated to this project? (Resources mean prior expenditures and commitments made.)

❑ Who has been assigned to be part of the team? What are their roles and responsibilities. (The more members, the higher the priority.)

❑ What have you already accomplished on this project? (Where are we in the project timeline?)

When you understand and align with commitments and allocated resources to maximize the existing investment, you create more value and a foster a cohesive customer connection.

Deadline

A deadline is the best priority indicator. It's fundamental to every deal.

> No DEADLINE, NO DEAL.

There are two types of deadlines: *internal* and *external*.

Internal Deadlines

Internal deadlines get set by the strategist, the person keeping score with KPIs. There's a high probability of hitting that deadline or someone's dead – their career takes a hit. When the deadline looms or there's an emergency, companies pay extra to expedite a solution. For example, overnight delivery costs 20-30 times more when compared to first class mail service. Faster costs more.

Understanding internal deadlines lets you judge priority and decide how to allocate sales resources.

External Deadlines

External deadlines we put on the prospect.

"If you order before the end of the month, I can knock off an additional 10 percent."

You always give away margin when using an external deadline. An external deadline attempts to alter the prospect priorities by trading budget for urgency. For high-consideration offerings, this rarely works to the seller's advantage, instead tipping your hand to show the buyer how low you'll go. And when they're ready to place the order, they'll want the same deal, and will probably hold out until you give it to them.

Don't offer discounts in exchange for an earlier order. It screws up margins, teaches prospects to expect discounts, and rarely brings in the deal sooner.

Exceptions to the no discounts rule:

1. You hold excess inventory (products, labor, empty calendar dates, perishable offerings) and need to move product now. When the overstock is gone, so is the deal.

2. You have an impending price increase and offer to sell at the current price now.

Smart Deadline Questions

Uncover deadlines with these smart questions:
- ❑ When does this need to be in place? (Installation deadline.)
- ❑ When do you want to start? (Availability deadline.)
- ❑ When do your people need to be trained? (Team readiness deadline.)
- ❑ What has to happen before you can begin? (Gating factor to the deadline.)

The response to the last question uncovers if there are things you can do to accelerate the deal. Perhaps you can clear the way with your products or services. Here's how:

"You said that before you can start, you must _____. I've got good news! We can do that as part of the project."

Notice that the question *not* to ask is, "When will you make the decision?" The answer to this is much more accurately determined from deadline questions. Besides, they've already decided, they haven't yet made the commitment.

Now that you understand their priorities, you can learn about what creates value for them.

Uncovering Criteria: What Prospects Find Valuable

Their criteria determine how they'll choose. It identifies what they find valuable, what they're willing to pay for. Criteria identifies *who* will do this and *how* they'll get it done, defining the deployment *tactics*.

Do you have control over your prospect's criteria?

Yes! You have much control through smart questions, education, and consulting. You and your team know more about the solutions available than your prospect. You invest time in training and study that they don't. Although you may be biased toward your product, your insights and knowledge have real value.

Prospect Education Influences Criteria

Consider this: if your prospects knew everything you know about your products, would they buy anything else?

If the answer is yes, you need to find a new product, right now.

If the answer is no, then your highest and best sales action is to offer education.

I discovered this as a young man selling for Hewlett-Packard (HP) back in the days when they were a test and measurement company (now Agilent and Keysight) that also sold computers. I'd run prospects through a two-hour training session that showed them how to solve their problem with my product. It wasn't a demo, it was a fun, interactive, hands-on session where they learned how to use the product, solve their measurement problems, and experience success. The training took away the fear, uncertainty, and doubt and left them confident and enthusiastic. The result: 80 percent would buy from me. The other 20 percent couldn't because of political reasons: their boss had committed to the competition.

In this experience, I learned a very important sales lesson about high-consideration, mission critical products. Simply this:

> THE MOST DANGEROUS THING TO YOUR COMPETITION
> IS A CUSTOMER WHO'S EDUCATED.

Education became my secret weapon. I taught my prospects how to choose my products and so grew my territory 100 percent per year three years in a row.

Education continues to be the cornerstone strategy for all disruptive sales activities. In today's market, you can quickly become a leader by offering training videos, breakfast briefings, lunch and learns, webinars, day-long strategy sessions, user groups, and so forth.

Smart Criteria Questions

Ask prospects questions about what brings them value and how they'll judge who is the best choice for achieving their objective.

❑ How will you know who to choose?

❑ All things being equal, who do you want to work with? Why?

❑ How will you determine value?

These next six questions explore their current criteria and help them expand their view of what's possible, potentially removing your competitors from the running.

1. "What are you using (or considering) now?"
   This question identifies what they've found valuable, so far. Even if they mention a hated competitor, don't flinch. You must understand their current thought process to align with their motivations.

2. "What do you like best about it?"
   Write down their answers. What they like best are key criteria and you've got to deliver them. Ask, "What else..." until they say, "That's it." You must get to all of the reasons why they like their current selection before proceeding, otherwise they will defend their choice and move into resistance, destroying the conversation flow.

3. "What do you like least about it?"
   Once they finish bragging about how bright they were for making their choice, they are psychologically able to complain. Write down their answers. Ask, "What else..." until they say, "That's it." Their answers are the anti-criteria, what they want to avoid and eliminate. If you can deliver what they like and avoid what they don't like, you're substantially closer to displacing the competition.

4. "If you could have things any way you wanted, what would you change?"

A magical question, it allows the prospect to expand their vision of what's possible, dreaming of a better outcome beyond what they're expecting from their current choice. If you can make their dreams come true, you become the desirable choice. Ask, "What else…" until they say, "That's it."

5. "If you could do that, what would it mean to you and your team?"

   This question turns the dream into reality, identifying the value when the dream comes true. This helps them pivot to a new possibility by making the new potential part of their identity. Ask, "What else…" until they say, "That's it."

6. "What would motivate you to change your mind?"

   This question makes them identify the circumstances in which they could abandon their current choice and make a different one. You've walked them through a question sequence that triggers a change of mind, if it's possible. Ask, "What else…" until they say, "That's it."

To make these six questions work you must do three things:

1. Use these specific words in the specific order. Vocabulary is important. Put this list of questions by your phone and use them until they become second nature.

2. Ask, "What else…" until they say, "That's it." You want to get out all of their answers for that question before you proceed, or you risk destroying the psychological flow.

3. Do not make any statements while asking the six questions. This is the time for diagnosis, not prescription. Take verbatim notes so that you can play back their answers when it comes time to make a compelling presentation, showing you listened, you understand, and you can help.

Do Your Research

Create additional context through research of the prospect company including customer feedback and review sources, on-line customer forums, annual reports, mission statements, and competitive gaps that you can solve.

Presenting to Their Motivation

When it's time for your presentation, start with, "Based on what you've told me so far..." and discuss the answers to the questions asked in context to the solution you recommend.

> ADULTS DON'T ARGUE WITH THEIR OWN DATA.

This methodology produces the best results of any I've experienced. Why? Because I know what they find valuable and what they don't find valuable, in their own words, and only discuss what I have that most closely matches what they have articulated to me.

Objection Bypass

The more of their criteria you use in the product-focused conversation, the more they feel that you have what they're looking for. Because you understood their motivation and mapped it to your offering, there will be no resistance and no objections. The natural next step becomes the prospect saying yes.

Chapter Summary

- Old sales methods don't work for high-consideration sales situations.
- Prospect motivation and your relationship are the most critical part of your sales success.
- Prospect motivation comes from their objectives, priorities, and criteria. Your value propositions have no meaning until they align with prospect motivation.

❑ Research and smart questions uncover prospect motivation.

❑ You have no control over objective and priorities, but you can influence criteria through education.

Ask Yourself

❑ The last time I lost a deal, what was the issue: prospect motivation, relationship, or the product?

❑ How can I pivot away from product pitches to a prospect motivation assessment methodology?

❑ When was the last time I was persuaded by a salesperson to buy something I resisted? If so, it was a low-consideration, low-risk purchase. What makes me think I can persuade an executive with this method when it doesn't work on me?

Ask Your Team

❑ The last time you lost a deal, what was the issue: prospect motivation, relationship, or the product?

❑ When you talk about the product what happens? When you talk about the prospect's needs, what happens? How can you adjust your talk track to take advantage of this reality?

❑ When was the last time you were persuaded by a salesperson to buy something you resisted? If so, it was a low-consideration, low-risk purchase. What makes you think that you can persuade an executive with this method when it doesn't work on you?

Action Plan

❑ Adapt the smart questions to your sales process.

❑ Use the sales success model to troubleshoot sales issues.

❑ Refuse to talk about products until you understand prospect motivation to eliminate objections and enhance the relationship.

Chapter 7:
Pivot Factor –
From Low-Consideration
to High-Consideration
Sales Strategy

Everybody has a purchase approval limit. You do. I do. Every prospect does. Every deal you've ever done has. Below that approval limit, the buyer can make a decision without consulting anyone else and without defending their decision, making for a speedy sale. Above that limit, the decision process gets more complex and lengthy.

You must adapt your marketing and sales tactics depending on customer approval limits and their concerns for risk.

The Purchase Limit

For business-to-consumer sales, personal limits may be set by spending habits, available cash on hand, and agreed-upon limits set with a life partner. The amount can be set by the daily spending limit for a debit card and ATM withdrawal, one's available credit, or a preapproved limit for large purchases such as a house, car, boat, or appliances.

For example, my wife and I make joint decisions on purchases above a certain limit. Even for routine budgeted expenses, we've agreed on those limits in advance so that we can control cash flows. I'm sure it's the same for you.

> SELLING ABOVE ONE'S PURCHASE LEVEL AUTHORITY
> EXTENDS THE SALES CYCLE.

For business-to-business sales, personal approval limits may be set by department history, executive mandate, role, and budget constraints. This often varies by business size and economic situations – when times get tough, limits plummet.

Small business owners usually demand approval for all purchases. Midsize business managers may allow departmental purchase approval of several thousand dollars to tens of thousands of dollars. Large companies, counterintuitively, often have lower approval thresholds.

I worked with a Fortune 100 company whose CEO reviewed every expenditure over $100k. Under the advice of our contacts, we just kept the project phases and invoices under that level.

Purchase limits can be contextual, differing for various purchase classes. For example, a routine purchase may have one limit and a one-time purchase may have a lower approval limit.

The Perceived Purchase Risk

A purchase can be considered risky when it involves a new vendor, a new product or service, or when there's a high failure cost. When selling a disruptive product, you'll be perceived as risky, so this principle becomes important to your success selling technology.

> DISRUPTIVE PRODUCTS FEEL RISKY TO NEW BUYERS.

Perceived risk causes sales resistance and purchase delay as the buyer considers risk/reward ratios, risk mitigation strategies, and risk costs. You are at psychological odds with the buyer because you pit your confidence against their fear. Until you can help them through their fear, or you have a trusted relationship with them, their fear wins.

Branding reduces perceived risk and fear because of prior satisfactory experience with the brand. If your customer trusts your brand, personal or corporate, perceived risk declines and the sales cycle accelerates. Tying a new, disruptive product to an existing brand decreases, but may not eliminate, perceived risk.

High-Consideration Versus Low-Consideration Purchase

Combining your customer's approval limits and perceived purchase risk determines whether a purchase is a high-consideration or low-consideration action. Purchases above their limit or high perceived risk makes the purchase a high consideration situation. Both high risk and above their approval limit indicates a very high consideration purchase and an extremely difficult sale situation. Below their limit and low perceived risk makes it a low consideration purchase. Low consideration sales can be made fast, in seconds to a few days.

Purchase Approval Limits and Perceived Risk Determine if a Purchase is Low Consideration or High Consideration

High consideration purchases require extensive analysis, consultation, and consensus of the approval team. The more levels of an organization that get included, the longer the cycle.

If the board of directors gets involved, it may take several 90-day board meeting cycles to get approval. High consideration sales can take months or years, a painful situation for a sales rep paid on monthly commission or quarterly goals.

Stop Thinking Sales Cycle, Start Thinking Consideration Cycle

Historically, we've discussed deal timing in terms of sales cycle with high consideration deals being a long cycle. I recommend that you stop talking about sales cycle time because how long it takes to close a deal is actually a function of how well you guide your customer through their consideration cycle. The length of the sale gets set by how well you manage their need for purchase approval and risk mitigation.

> YOUR SALES CYCLE IS BASED ON HOW QUICKLY YOU CAN MOVE YOUR CUSTOMER FROM CAUTIOUS TO CONFIDENT.

Instead of thinking in terms of time, think of it in terms of what's needed to move the decision-making team to confidence, the threshold of every sale. Now you can choose strategies and deploy tactics to get to confidence, psychologically and fiscally, as quickly as possible. Let's consider some tactics to speed the deal.

Scope Out Their Limit

Find out what they can approve with smart questions:
❑ "What price have you approved for something like this in the past?"
❑ "Who has to approve of this purchase before you can commit?"
❑ "At what price point do you need to get purchase approval?"

❑ "Do you need to break this into multiple invoices or payments to fit this into your signature authority?"

❑ "What's your signature limit?"

Who Approves Over-Limit Purchases?

Discover who's in the approval chain. This information becomes valuable for expanding opportunities and future deals.

❑ "At what price point do you need to get someone else involved? Who is that?"

❑ "Who has approved a purchase like this before? Are they available to review this?"

❑ "What is their purchase approval level?"

❑ "To whom do they need to justify their approval decision?"

❑ "What criteria do they use to make the approval?"

❑ "Under what circumstances can they approve more budget?"

Increase the Limit

You can increase approval limits by helping them find additional and alternative ways to pay for the purchase. Accept multiple purchase orders, each within their signature authority. Provide a monthly or quarterly subscription, financing, payment terms, offer trade-in allowances to expand their limit. Use coupons, rebates, referral bonuses, and other ways for the customer to earn as they buy, effectively increasing their budget limit.

Get creative by identifying other internal budget sources, perhaps other departments or equally motivated colleagues.

Scope Out Their Concerns for Risk

Use smart questions to understand their fears. Old school sales trainer's heads would explode if they knew I was telling you to explore why the prospect might not want to buy. But then, they didn't understand high-consideration sales situations.

❑ "What concerns do you have about this purchase?"

❑ "What would cause you to hold off on this?"

❑ "What risks do you consider as you make your decision?"

❑ "On a scale of one to ten, how confident are you about this? What do you need to move that up a point?"

❑ "If you need for me to guarantee any one thing about this, what would it be?" (You don't have to guarantee it, but the question reveals the concern that must be addressed for the deal to proceed.)

❑ "What have others warned you about as you consider this purchase? What was their experience that triggered the warning?"

❑ "Who do you have to assure about this decision? What do they consider when making a judgment?"

❑ "To whom do you need to defend your decision? What criteria do they use to decide?"

❑ "What risks do they consider as they make their decision?"

❑ "What's the worst thing that could happen if you decided to buy and something went wrong? What if we could guarantee that didn't happen?"

❑ "What would it cost if you didn't make a decision?"

❑ "What would it be worth to decide to move forward?"

Mitigate Risk

Help them eliminate or mitigate risk so they can safely decide to buy. You can use satisfaction guarantees, product warranties, and risk reversal strategies – "If you're not happy, I'll refund your money and you keep what we shipped to you." You can offer insurance and performance guarantees.

Think of every reason why a customer would feel risk and look for a way to make the risk go away.

Eliminate Buyer's Remorse

An important part of the disruptive sales process is allowing the customer to examine and dismiss their perceived risk elements. Don't try to pitch them through their fears (an old school method), but instead invite them to bring them up and then help them lay them to rest.

This is another application of "Customer's don't argue with their own data." When they decide it's not a risk now, then it's not likely going to be a risk in the future. This process eliminates buyer's remorse, where after the sale they feel regret or fear.

In today's review driven, social media world, buyer's remorse can quickly ruin your brand. Avoiding buyer's remorse is worth the time and effort, ensuring you have positive word-of-mouth instead of having to clean up an unhappy customer experience.

Bought Versus Sold

Are the products you offer *bought* or *sold*? The difference: a customer-initiated purchase indicates a *bought* product and a sales person initiated purchase indicates a *sold* product.

When a customer you don't have a relationship with calls you with to place order, they're buying. You didn't do any selling to make the deal. You may have done marketing to alert them that you offered it for sale, but there was no sales activity on your part. They made the decision on their own.

If you have an inside sales team, they probably don't do much selling, yet they're very good at taking orders and helping customers with a product configuration. If they suggest additional items to customers – cross selling – or the customer accepts their recommendation for a better, costlier product – upselling – then they've *sold*. I recommend an inside team be salaried unless they upsell or cross sell, and then only commissioned on that part of the transaction.

> ### ALL NEW TECHNOLOGY GETS SOLD.
> ### ALL OLD TECHNOLOGY GETS BOUGHT.

All new technology must be sold. Prospects don't know the solution exists so must be introduced to it and taught the value and outcome it delivers. Over time, they associate the outcome they desire with that technology and begin to buy it on their own volition. A sales professional is very valuable in the first situation and has much less value in the second.

Selling Across the Chasm

Geoffrey Moore wrote about technology life cycles in his book *Crossing the Chasm* in 1999. If you've studied any marketing, you're familiar how he took the concept of the impact of time on customer adoption of new technology and identified changing marketing issues as a product matures in the marketplace.

In my interpretation, the study is about the risk profile of customers, whether they view the new technology as high consideration or low consideration.

The first few customers (tech seekers) search for new technology, so *buy* it without much concern for risk, because they want the latest and greatest because of their search for thought leadership or bragging rights. For this group, all you need to do is let them know it's available and they'll line up to buy. Reminds you of iPhone purchasers.

The next wave of customers (early adopters) must be *sold* the product, as they have an unmet need pressing them to find for new answers and are willing to take the risk on a new potential solution. Moore's chasm comes from needing to make the switch from taking orders from hungry customers to finding prospects who value the outcome the technology delivers.

The next wave of customers (leading) must be *sold* the product to help them overcome their concerns for risk of the new, unknown, and potentially unproven. To summarize, the left half of the curve indicate mostly high consideration sales situations where the technology gets sold.

The right half of the curve is where the technology gets bought. Customers are lagging because they didn't have the need earlier, get recommendations from others, and generally feel the purchase is now low consideration, either because of the low risk or lower price that now falls within their purchase authority.

Use the Right Sales Strategy

Now that you understand how to determine if your customer will view this deal as high or low consideration, you can now select the right method to engage with them.

> THE BIGGEST MISTAKE IN SALES TODAY IS USING LOW CONSIDERATION SALES METHODS FOR HIGH CONSIDERATION DEALS.

"Mark! I can't understand it. I've been so successful in sales, and now I can't close a single deal."

Ken, my coaching client couldn't figure out why his time-tested sales tactics stopped working.

If you've been in sales for a while or if you manage a sales team, you've experienced this situation.

Isn't sales, sales?

Don't sales skills transfer from product to product?

Can't someone who can sell ice cubes to Eskimos sell anything?

You know the answer: No!

> CURRENT SALES SUCCESS DOESN'T GUARANTEE FUTURE SUCCESS.

But, why not? Why doesn't sales success transfer?

These questions triggered my quest for understanding the situation and after three years of questions, conversations, research, and testing you're about to discover the answer I've found.

> ### HOW PEOPLE BUY IS CONTEXTUAL,
> ### SO SALES TECHNIQUES MUST BE CONTEXTUAL.

Customers take different approaches to how they buy based on if it's a high-consideration or low-consideration purchase. Ken was using one successful customer journey experience to attempt a very different customer journey and it failed. It wasn't his fault. He used what he found successful out of context and it didn't work.

I've discovered there are four fundamental methods for marketing and sales. Let's explore them now.

Tactical Versus Strategic

We can take any product or service and place it on a continuum ranging from tactical to strategic.

Tactical products are purchased to perform a task, strategic products are purchased to accomplish a mission.

> ### TASKS ARE SHORT-TERM DEMANDS
> ### AND MISSIONS ARE LONG-TERM PLANS.

Tactical Purchases

Tactical purchases satisfy a day-to-day demand. Failure has low impact. If someone makes a bad decision, it can be rapidly fixed, with plenty of alternative replacement vendors clamoring for the business.

Characteristics of a Tactical Purchase:

- ❏ Purchased to perform a task
- ❏ Usually bought rather than sold
- ❏ Relatively simple product
- ❏ Commodity item
- ❏ Low consideration purchase
- ❏ Low risk purchase
- ❏ Short sales cycle
- ❏ Short product life or service contract
- ❏ Consumable item
- ❏ Considered a cost or expense
- ❏ Mass produced
- ❏ Volume pricing
- ❏ Lower price point
- ❏ Minimal sales skills required
- ❏ Does not require a high-cognitive capacity sales person and supervisory team

Customers buy tactical products and services to perform a task that's short term, with immediate impact, and may have limited future impact. Only occasionally are tactical purchases sold through a sales person's actions because the price and profit margins often preclude paying commissions.

They are low-consideration purchases with low risk. If the customer makes the wrong choice, it's just an inconvenience and it can be replaced with low cost and little effort.

> "IT'S IMPORTANT TO KNOW THE DIFFERENCE
> BETWEEN AN INCONVENIENCE AND A CATASTROPHE."
> – BRUCE LEE

The vendor incurs little financial risk-taking returns and refunding money to a dissatisfied customer.

The sales cycle (consideration => decision => commitment) tends to be relatively short once the customer decides to purchase, taking seconds, minutes, days, or occasionally weeks to select a vendor.

Customers view a tactical purchase as an expense or a cost. It's often a recurring purchase.

Products or services are mass produced with prices set to move volumes of product.

Sales skills required are minimal, usually knowing product location in the retail outlet or in a catalog.

"Do you have energy shots?"

"Yes, at the register."

A slight increase in sales staff product knowledge can lead to a substantial increase in sales volume.

"You might try this new energy product. Customers tell me it lasts all day."

Cognitive capacity of the sales and supervisory team need not be high, usually operating at minimum wage or slightly above.

Strategic Purchases

Customers purchase strategic products to perform a mission that has long-range importance to them. There are fewer acceptable vendors. Failure has high impact and often can't be rapidly resolved.

Characteristics of a Strategic Purchase:
- Purchased to perform a mission
- Usually sold rather than bought
- Relatively complex product
- High consideration purchase
- High risk purchase
- Long sales cycle
- Long product life or service contract (durable)
- Considered an investment

❑ Custom made or customized
❑ Relatively higher price
❑ Value pricing
❑ Skilled sales team required
❑ Requires a high-cognitive capacity sales person and supervisory team

Customers purchase strategic products for a mission with long term, future impact. It may have limited immediate impact.

Strategic products tend to be complex that require significant consideration to make the best choice. It's a high-risk purchase: if they don't get it right, there is serious impact and they may not have sufficient resources to select another option. Sales professionals are almost always involved because of the complexity of selecting, configuring, and deploying the purchase, meaning the product is sold versus bought.

The sales cycle can be quite long, taking weeks, months, or even years to complete.

What's Your Product Position?

You can map every product and service you buy and sell on this continuum.

For example: fast-food restaurants perform the tactical function of suppressing hunger. You're driving down the road, you see their sign, you sense hunger, you stop and make the hunger go away. They're not in the business of nutrition or a fine dining experience.

Your favorite restaurant, the one you call for reservations when celebrating, has a strategic function. Satiating hunger is secondary to the dining and celebration experience.

Asking your true love to marry you at MacDonald's may not go as well as proposing at Capital Grill.

Who's Involved in the Decision

The second continuum is how many people get involved in making the decision.

If one person makes the choice and does not have to defend their choice, the sale happens at their decision-making speed based on their priorities and criteria (much more on this starting on page 63).

The more people involved, the longer it takes to make a decision because of the exponentially increasing complexity of satisfying and aligning each person's priorities and criteria.

> SALES CLOSE FAST UNDER TWO CONDITIONS:
> ONLY ONE PERSON'S CHOICE MATTERS
> OR IT'S AN EMERGENCY.

For example, when you're eating alone, only you need to choose the restaurant. When you dine with others, it's way more complex.

"Where do you want to eat?"

"Doesn't matter."

You suggest restaurant after restaurant until "doesn't matter" identifies their preference. That's why Cheesecake Factory is often a good choice because of their War-and-Peace-sized menu.

You're laughing because it's true.

> A CUSTOMER CONFUSED CANNOT CHOOSE.

What causes this phenomenon is *choice overload*. When someone has too many options, they can't decide. This happens when you offer a catalog of products or a portfolio pitch expecting for the customer to know what to choose. While this might work for a technical buyer who knows what they're looking for, it doesn't work for complex products and services.

The Customer Buying Matrix

When we arrange these two continua in a four-quadrant model, we get a new understanding of marketing and sales.[32]

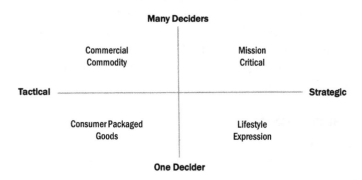

The Customer Buying Matrix: Purchase Type and Decider Count Determines How to Market and Sell

The upper half of the model defines business-to-business sales and the lower half defines business-to-consumer sales.

Commercial Commodity

Commercial commodities are undifferentiated products and services. The average customer can't tell the difference between a print out from an equivalent computer printer or differentiate from the virtually identical selection of Chromebook computers.

---

[32] In this book, we'll explore the quadrants germane to selling I.T. For an in-depth discussion of this model, read my book, *Selling Disruption*. http://SellingDisruption.com

Vendors attempt differentiation through features, advantages, and benefits hoping to make their price stick through increased value.

This sales scenario is where you find purchasing departments, which exist to turn every vendor into a commodity in an attempt to force the decision to lowest price. For that reason, this is the lowest margin quadrant, usually in the single digit margin percentages. Customers buying in this quadrant exhibit no loyalty, they're after the best price for what's considered to be a consumable or relatively short-life product.

Overt decision criterion is based on best *price*, but the covert criteria is reliable *delivery*.

Consumer Packaged Goods

Consumer Packaged Goods (CPG) are anything in Wal-Mart, fundamentally mass-market retail. They are mass produced products that consumers purchase based on immediate need. Fast Moving Consumer Goods (FMCG) are low-cost consumables that require no purchase decisions, such as fountain soft drinks, fast food, auto fuel, and convenience store products.

This quadrant is where the four P's of marketing (price, product, promotion, place) work along with traditional FAB-based (features, advantages, benefits) selling. The consumer may compare packages of competing products and will make their decision in seconds based on the product label claims, past brand experience, and recommendations from friends.

Overt decision criterion is based on *convenience* and *price*. Covert decision criterion is based on *habit*. To disrupt CPG buyers requires habit pattern interrupt.

Lifestyle Expression

Lifestyle expression products support a person's self identity and define their tribe. For example, your choice of lifestyle determines where you live, where you send your children to school, where you buy clothing, what church you attend, and what car you drive.

The highest margins are found in the Lifestyle Expression quadrant, with jewelry running at 400 to 1,000 percent markup, clothing at 300 percent, and make up and fragrance in the 1,000 percent range.

Make a choice outside of your usual self identity and you'll discover that you lose old friends and make new ones. In this quadrant, recommendations from trusted friends has enormous impact on your decision-making process. Influencer marketing becomes critical for success. Customers tend to select and support a brand with strong loyalty because that brand becomes part of their identity. This is why "fluffy" identity-focused marketing works in this quadrant: you're selling lifestyle expression, not product.

Apple disrupted the mobile phone market by moving commodity tech products into the lifestyle expression quadrant, raking in massive profits and owning the bulk of the market revenue.

Key decision criteria are based on personal *identity, culture*, and *values*. The covert criterion is buyer *prestige*.

Mission Critical

Mission critical products determine the efficiency and flexibility of an organization. Choose poorly and the company may perish. Decisions of this magnitude become the domain of the executive team, who are tasked with the organization's success.

Mission critical products include building location, business systems (such as Oracle, SAP, Microsoft, HP, IBM, Dell, NetApp, etc.) and vendors who support those systems.

Mission critical purchases tend to be long-term decisions and investments with much inertia. Once the choice gets made, it won't change for a while.

Sell mission critical products by mapping the buying team's objectives, priorities, and criteria (OPC) to your offering. Products are usually too complex to use FAB-based product pitches in the absence of understanding customer's desired outcome. There are too many people involved to satisfy every priority and criteria with a canned pitch. You run a big risk of creating too many objections if you do.

Margins are substantially higher than commercial commodity and customers become quite loyal.

Overt reason to purchase is desired *outcome*. The covert reason is vendor *trust* and relationship: show that you can deliver their desired outcome and then some, you win.

This quadrant is where you want to be selling.

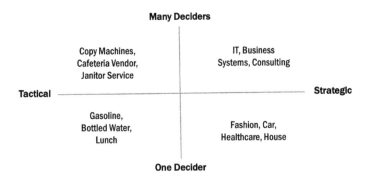

The Customer Buying Matrix: Product Examples

Value-Based Decisions

Products and services on the left side of the model are considered commodities by the buyer: while they may have a brand preference, almost any brand will do. The purchase is often based on function versus price. Customers will tolerate lower performance for a lower price, but may not choose increased performance for a higher price. This is why contrasting product ranges, such as *good, better*, and *best* can facilitate decisions.

> ## CONTRAST CREATES CLARITY.

If the buyer makes a mistake, they can fix it quickly and with little, if any, loss. On this side of the model, purchase criteria centers around *value*. The lower the decision risk, the faster the decision.

Competitors try to lure buyers away from brand preference by offering the same outcome at a lower price or more desired outcome at the same price.

Values-Based Decisions

Products and services on the right side of the model are considered special: they aren't bought often so require careful consideration. A person's *values* come into play as they make their choice. The choice becomes based on how the purchase supports the business model and culture.

> ## VALUES TRUMPS VALUE, EVERY TIME.

If the buyer makes a mistake, it becomes costly to fix the problem and may be impossible to recover. The higher the decision risk, the slower the decision.

The competitive battle is based on achieving desired outcome and who becomes more trusted. In this half of the model, discounting is uncommon because price is rarely the tie-breaker. If there is a discount, it's negotiated, not offered unasked.

For example, does your favorite makeup or cologne ever go on sale? Nope. You might get a gift with purchase, which is a sample of what they want you to buy next. Does Apple discount their latest products? Nope. And you'd probably judge it to be a knock off if they did.

Customers Choose Vendors that Culturally Align

Your corporate culture ultimately determines who will buy from you. The entire customer experience from marketing, to sales, to customer support, to product performance must align with the buyer's culture and values.

If you fail, you'll never know because customers just stop returning your calls. If you press them for a reason, they'll say, "It just isn't a good fit." Your team blames the customer instead of themselves.

If your team makes excuses for low performance, you've got a serious culture issue. More than one company has perished because of cultural misalignment: their marketing promised a desirable experience and the sales team delivered a subpar one.

> YOUR SALES CULTURE HAS MORE IMPACT ON YOUR SUCCESS
> THAN YOU CAN IMAGINE.

Without every employee in alignment with customer culture, you run the risk of your people inadvertently sabotaging customer relationships.

How Selling Tactics Change

Selling tactics for each quadrant are quite different. If you have a broad portfolio, break your offering into commercial commodity and mission critical categories.

Commercial Commodity	Mission Critical
1. Appointment	1. Research
2. Pitch (FAB)	2. Appointment
3. Overcome Objections	3. Assessment (OPC)
4. Discount	4. Report of Findings
5. Close	5. Recommendations
6. Deliver	6. Phased Rollout

Consumer Packaged Goods	Lifestyle Expression
Point of Purchase (FAB)	Marketing
Sampling & Self Service	Get Acquainted (OPC)
4Ps of Marketing: Product,	Recommendation
Placement, Position, Price	Trial/Gift with Purchase
	Delivery

The Customer Buying Matrix: Selling Tactics

How to Sell Commercial Commodity Products

Sell commercial commodities with an inside sales team, on line, and through catalogs. They usually have insufficient margins to use a dedicated outside sales force unless the deals are big.

Use FAB-based sales *pitches* to allow the customer to self-identify their desired outcome at the price they want. Make sure that your sales talk tracks include details that would satisfy the KPIs of your decision maker. Only present after doing at least a cursory conversation about objectives, priorities, and criterial.

Product comparison matrices and decision trees can help facilitate and accelerate the buying process.

Most of the sales strategies you've been taught live in this quadrant, as they've been product focused and FAB based.

How to Sell Mission Critical Products

Sell mission critical products through an *assessment* strategy to understand the buying team's OPC, deliver your report of findings, make recommendations, and deliver in a phased rollout.

This approach exploits the concept, "Customers never argue with their own data" presenting what they find motivating and in alignment with their culture and priorities. A phased deployment approach minimizes risk because they can adjust the plan if a phase doesn't go to expectations.

Which Selling Method to Choose?

How can you tell which method to use? If multiple people need to say yes, you'll need an assessment. If one person decides, you may wish to use the commercial commodity method.

The exception to this recommendation is if you want to disrupt your market by moving your product position from one quadrant to another, either by your go-to-market strategy or by price reductions to where the typical buyer can make a solo purchase decision.[33]

Business Assessments Close Deals Fast

Business case assessments provide a methodical and formal approach to understanding customer objectives, priorities, and criteria from the bottom to the top of the data value hierarchy. It documents the objective desires, opportunities, risks, future value, and forecasts organizational needs in a *Report of Findings*.

Customer executives demand this type of formal review and willingly pay for expertise to speed the process and increase accuracy, insight, and foresight. Consulting companies charge large sums for this service. You might as well get in on the action for your customers of all sizes.

---

[33] If this is you, let's talk.

> ### A REPORT OF FINDINGS IS
> SUBSTANTIALLY MORE PERSUASIVE THAN ANY PROPOSAL
> BECAUSE THEY WON'T DISAGREE WITH THEIR OWN DATA.

Your technical and business acumen become evident and, in the process, executives perceive you to be relevant, valuable, and non-discretionary.

I've built dozens and dozens of business case tools for clients through the decades for marquis I.T. vendors.[34] Prosperous business partners use assessments as the key to their sales success. They always have substantial positive business impact on those who choose to use them.

What's Been Your Assessment Experience?

Consider this: when you do a paid business case assessment, your close rate on follow-on purchases should run in the 80 percent plus range. Competition will be very low or non-existent because of the trust built during the assessment process. Margins come in substantially higher because you deliver value-based fees commensurate with the customer's outcome. Deals close much faster because the customer has all of the information they need to make a defensible decision and can rearrange their priorities appropriately. You've done all of the work for them. When they agree, they'll buy.

When you quote products to new customers, your close rate is low, your margins razor thin, deals take time, and you battle competition galore.

Why are you quoting products? It's a bad business model, you're wasting your resources, and it's unsustainable given the business model pivots. Stop it!

---

[34] Want me to build one for your company? Let's talk!

Not All Assessments are Created Equal

Notice I discussed *paid* business case assessments. If your customer is unwilling to pay for it, there's no skin in the game, they are price sensitive, or they're at the wrong level in the organization and therefore your success declines substantially. I strongly advise against a free assessment unless you can identify a clear strategic advantage in doing so.

Many assessments focus on existing technology with a goal to rip and replace. This isn't enough. You've got to include the business issues by assessing the data creators and data consumer's future demands and vision. To win, you've got to deliver the complete business exam, not just a cursory technology review.

> YOU CAN OFTEN SELL A BUSINESS CASE ASSESSMENT
> EVEN WHEN THERE'S NO TECHNOLOGY BUDGET.

The good news: an executive can agree to a business case assessment even though the CIO may not currently be in the market for technology because the CEO values foresight, using your observations to plot their future.

Chapter Summary

❑ Your sales cycle depends on your customer's perception of risk in context of their signature authority level. The higher the perceived risk and the more people involved, the longer the sales cycle.

❑ I.T. sales require high consideration from the buying team, so require a different sales method.

❑ Business-to-business sales can be defined as commercial commodity or mission critical, requiring different approaches to marketing and sales.

❑ Business case assessments accelerate success when selling mission critical products and services.

Ask Yourself

- ❑ Do I see the value in selling and delivering business case assessments?
- ❑ Am I willing to pivot to a business case assessment focused practice?
- ❑ What is my mix of commercial commodities versus mission critical offerings?
- ❑ How can I pivot my sales and tech delivery team to deliver business case assessments?

Ask Your Team

- ❑ What has been your experience with technical assessments?
- ❑ What has been your experience with business case assessments?
- ❑ What do you think would happen if we pivoted from quoting products to only doing projects based on a business case assessment?
- ❑ How do you see yourself participating in a business model like this?

Action Plan

- ❑ Research vendors for business case assessment tools.
- ❑ Design your pricing structure for business case assessments.
- ❑ Redesign your sales and support compensation structure to support a business case assessment business model.
- ❑ Connect with the MSP to BSP community for assessment resources and training at MSPtoBSP.com.

Chapter 8:
Pivot Factor –
From Data Acumen
to Business Acumen

As you pivot from data curation acumen to business acumen, your experience running a business becomes more valuable. With wide-spread and never-ending business model pivots, your insights and foresights about business rules implementation in I.T. becomes your differentiator and unique value proposition.

Once customers understand what you and your team can do, you'll always be invited to a seat at the table to discuss business strategy and you become a trusted business partner.

You know many experts in data curation. How many people do you know who are business experts? Probably not many. Time for that to change. It's time for you to be a business expert and have a team full of them. When you're selling to the upper levels of the data value hierarchy, you've got to speak their language.[35]

In this chapter, let's examine the seven business pillars to review what you need to consider to up-level your business acumen.

The Seven Business Pillars

Business expertise isn't easy, but it is simple. I've identified seven critical business pillars that uphold a sustainable, scalable, profitable, and salable business. They define the seven areas of business acumen. When you understand the strategies

---

[35] Want to attend an event that brings your business acumen up to speed fast? Consider the Executive Strategy Summit. Details at http://ExecutiveStrategySummit.com

for each pillar and how to measure success in each area, you can delegate responsibility to direct a complex organization without having to do everything yourself, or worse, perform poorly in a number of the pillars.

Expect problems in a business when an executive abdicates responsibility for any of these pillars to someone without understanding of the key performance indicators (KPIs), knowing what questions to ask to understand desired outcomes, or lacking the skills to provide strategic direction.

> ### AN EXECUTIVE WILL NEVER AGREE TO A PROJECT THAT THEY DON'T KNOW HOW TO MANAGE.

While it's appropriate and sane to delegate sequence and tactics, the executive must be responsible for setting strategy and managing to KPIs, timelines, and milestones.

Consider these seven fundamental aspects of every business.

1. Products that Create Unique Value for the Target Market

The product is anything that the organization produces, services they deliver, or environment that they organize.

Every business must have a clearly defined market that identifies with them and their products.

> ### WHEN YOUR PRODUCT IS FOR EVERYBODY, YOU'LL FIND YOU'RE SELLING TO NOBODY.

The key take-away: organizations must target customers who identify with what they sell. You do this by aligning with customer values, tuning the product message directly to them by speaking their language, providing unique value, selling the way that they want to buy, and delivering their desired outcomes.

Customers select products that reflect their personal identity. Never has this been truer than today, illustrated by the vast product portfolios available from many different manufacturers.

This concept of identity also comes into play for government and education organizations. City and state governments choose business rules – tax incentives, mandates, technology, environment, and outreach – to encourage certain types of citizens and businesses to choose their locations. This is how they define community culture, their product.

> ## CUSTOMERS BUY TO SUPPORT AND UP-LEVEL THEIR SELF IDENTITY.

For example, Nevada has for decades offered a relaxed stance on gambling and other vices creating a booming economy. When other states offered lottery and other gaming opportunities, Nevada pivoted their business model to entertainment, meetings, and world-class restaurants, redefining their product. "What happens in Vegas, stays in Vegas" creates a liberal environment that lures conventioneers and vacationers. Little do most visitors realize that this slogan actually refers to gambling money, as tourists substantially understate how much they've lost and overstate how much they've won.

Being a viable BSP means understanding your customer's customer better than anyone else. Yes, this means someone on your team will do research because customers often can't do objective research.

Key performance indicators (KPIs) of product success include market penetration, speed of market adoption, level of disruption, maintaining product margin over time, etc.

Virtually every business demands a well thought out product development plan, fundamental to business model pivots.

2. Marketing that Triggers Relevant Conversations

Marketing is everything that you do before you have a meaningful customer conversation. It takes them on the journey from being unaware to aware, to interested, to asking for a conversation.

If your marketing doesn't trigger a relevant conversation, it's not marketing, it's a waste of money.

> WHEN YOU HAVE TO COLD CALL TO FIND CUSTOMERS,
> YOUR MARKETING IS BROKEN.

Relevance is the key. I can get you conversations all day long: "$100 gift card when you book an appointment!" All that happens is you waste time trying to persuade a non-decision maker into introducing you to their boss. Not going to happen.

The best marketing provides prospects with outcome-based education. It teaches customers how to buy what you sell.

One of the best books on marketing is *Guerrilla Marketing* by my co-author, the late, great Jay Conrad Levinson. Focusing on what works, Jay's words of wisdom are worth studying and implementing.

Every sustainable, scalable business has a formal marketing plan. These plans demand I.T. to implement, track, mine, and manage prospect data, which is why marketing buys more I.T. than the data center.

> YOU REAP IN SALES WHAT YOU SOW IN MARKETING.

Marketing KPIs include the number of conversations generated, the quality of the conversation (are those inquiring qualified), and the sales cycle time (where are customers in their purchase journey when they ask for a conversation.)

3. Sales that Facilitates Mutually Profitable Transactions

Sales is the customer-centered conversations that fill in the information gaps, organize the details, eliminate customer concerns, and make sure that you are the only desirable choice.

As you've learned in a prior chapter, only ten percent of sales success rests on the products or services. The rest is based on mapping customer motivation to the offering and building a trusted relationship.

The reason I use the word *facilitate* is because the notion of *closing* sales is false and narcissistic. Unless you have signature authority on your customer's bank account, there is only facilitation. I've only known one sales man who had that power.[36]

> THE DEAL CLOSES WHEN THE CUSTOMER'S READY AND NOT UNTIL.

Deals must be *mutually profitable* or someone is getting robbed and the relationship isn't sustainable. Your customers who buy mission critical products from you want you to be successful. They want you to stay in business because you are an important part of their business model. While they don't want to be gouged, they're willing to pay you a fair profit and expect you to cover your expenses on every project you undertake. If you sell in the Commercial Commodity quadrant, this may not be true as customers often try to get you to sell to them below your cost. They ask you to liquidate your company for their benefit. I never need a customer like that.

Part of the responsibility of sales is *forecasting*. This allows the rest of operations to get a handle on demand and assign resources to deliver. There's a difference between a pipeline and

---

[36] Outside of the scope of this book, I tell this story in my book, *Selling Disruption*. http://SellingDisruption.com

a forecast. A *pipeline* consists of prospects who have made a decision, moving toward making a commitment. A forecast is a customer with an internal deadline. If the customer doesn't have a deadline, it's not a deal, it's a wish. When working with high consideration sales, accurate forecasts become more important because of the magnitude of resources required to deliver the customer purchase.

Every sustainable, scalable, profitable, and salable business has a formal sales strategy, complete with a well-defined culture, formal sales methodology, sales management systems, and on-going sales reviews.

Sales KPIs include deal size, forecast accuracy, and sales and operating margins.

4. Service that Earns Customer Loyalty

Until your customer experiences you, there is no loyalty. When customers consider that they got what they paid for and nothing more, there is no loyalty, it was a fair exchange.

It's when customers feel that they got more than they paid for, usually in insight and foresight, that they feel like they hit the jackpot.

> UNTIL YOU DELIVER BEYOND WHAT A CUSTOMER EXPECTS
> AND PAYS FOR, THERE IS NO LOYALTY.

Customer service is the investment that you make in the next sale. You might consider it to be marketing to existing customers, a worthwhile investment because you'll make more money on the second transaction than you will the first.

Because of the perception of risk in high consideration purchases, your customers will likely first make a small purchase, preferring to have a phased deployment to manage and mitigate risk. Always be earning the right to sell the next phase of the deployment.

Customer service drives the most desirable of marketing activity, referrals. Yet, referrals are earned. Teach and motivate your customer service people to harvest referrals and they'll become one of the most profitable parts of your customer acquisition system.

Service KPIs include percentage of customers that repeat purchase, customer satisfaction scores, and the number of referrals generated.

5. Operations that Scale with Economic Cycles

We've just gone through an era where businesses crashed and burned because of an economic downturn. Many failed because they couldn't downsize fast enough. This is a case where efficiency failed and flexibility had real value, or would have.

> YOU CAN THRIVE IN BUSINESS DURING GOOD TIMES AND BAD IF YOU CAN FLEXIBLY SCALE WITH VARYING DEMAND.

Customers willingly pay slightly more for flexibility, including the ability to change how much they consume, what they consume, and when they consume it.

Savvy execs attempt to outsource as much of their production as they can, converting much of their fixed capital costs to variable operating expense.

Operations KPIs reflect the ability to make rapid changes and efficiency of the processes.

6. Finance that Controls Cash Flow and Funds the Future

Cash flow is king, as the old business mantra goes. Without a solid cash flow and working capital management system in place, including tying expenses to sales, a business operates with a risky business model.

This includes government and education organizations because they have to match cash outflow with tax and tuition revenue inflows. If they can't, they must borrow money bringing a whole new set of complexities, because the source of funds determines the business model.

> CASH FLOW IS KING. IF YOU WANT FULL CONTROL OF YOUR DESTINY, YOU'VE GOT TO SELF-FUND YOUR BUSINESS.

By embracing a primarily OpEx model, business can retain more earnings to fund growth, such as investing in new products, marketing, and sales.

A common long-term business challenge is declining margins over time as companies cut pricing in an attempt to compete with new market entrants. Many a successful company has crashed and burned when margins eroded and replacement products weren't ready. Helping your customers integrate product development with cash flow and funding management can substantially increase the probably of their long-term success.

Financial KPIs include cash flow levels, cash flow velocity, and operating capital levels and trends.

7. Culture that Upholds a Unique Brand Experience

Many companies underestimate the power of culture. Culture is the unspoken or codified business rules of conduct that defines how the company team behaves, how they treat each other, and ultimately how they treat customers. Culture determines the success of the chosen business model.

> CULTURE DETERMINES HOW WE TREAT EACH OTHER: EMPLOYEES, PROSPECTS, AND CUSTOMERS.

Culture overrules everything, whether it's defined, allowed, or tolerated. No matter what the mission statement or business rules, culture dominates the tone of business.

> CULTURE EATS STRATEGY FOR BREAKFAST.
> – PETER DRUCKER

Most entrepreneurial businesses start out with the founder's personal culture being the company culture. As the company grows, the founder hires people they know and so easily align with that undocumented culture. When the company grows beyond the founder's family and friends, they inadvertently hire people who don't share their same culture and the company starts to deviate as these new people begin to hire and manage to their personal culture.

The only way to keep this from happening is to define culture and have it reflected in the business model and business rules.[37] Culture ultimately defines the company's *brand*.

What is Branding?

Let's explore the concept of brand for a moment. Branding is more than a logo, color palate, or any other design element. Branding is the expectation of a certain experience.

> BRANDING DELIVERS THE PROMISE OF A CERTAIN EXPERIENCE,
> THEREFORE REDUCING PURCHASE RISK.

The history of branding goes back to the days when cattle ran free in the open range of the United States. Cattle owners

---

[37] One of the best examples of culture and brand definition comes from New York agency, DiMassimo Goldstein. Founder, Mark DiMassimo shares it with you at http://digobrands.com/digo-brands-a-culture/

would mark their herd with a hot branding iron. When the cowboys drove the livestock to market, buyers over time could identify which cattle had better pasture, better care, better water and therefore would taste superior. They would say, "I want that brand."

Branding is:

1. A customer *experience* that
2. They *value*
3. They willingly *pay* for
4. They want to *repeat*
5. Not *available* elsewhere
6. They'll *tell* others about.

If any of these six elements are missing, it's not a sustainable, scalable brand. Brand experience happens at every touch point a customer has with the company environment, products, and people.

Brand gets reinforced through the design of I.T. systems, ensuring that the team delivers the desired customer experience and offers ways of managing exceptions that indicate a potential business rule change. Systems with too much rigidity open the market to competition that can better respond to customer demands with reduced friction.

KPIs for culture can include customer satisfaction scores (yes, this is where this belongs), customer alignment with stated target customer goals, employee satisfaction scores, and personal satisfaction of the executive team.

How All This Fits Together

Identify the business pillars that you and your team need to master. It can be as easy as reading a book, taking a course, or hiring a business coach or consultant to fill in the blanks, identify your blind spots, and develop KPIs to monitor, manage, and improve your business.

When working with your customer, have conversations about the business pillars and how they measure and manage success with their KPIs. Look at how they implement the KPIs as business rules into their I.T. systems.

Consider offering your customers ideas on how to improve the KPIs with better business models and better culture, resulting in a sustainable, scalable, profitable, and ultimately salable business, becoming a valued business services partner.

Chapter Summary

❑ All successful organizations are built on the seven business pillars.

❑ The Seven Business Pillars:
   1. Products that create unique value for the target market
   2. Marketing that triggers relevant conversations
   3. Sales that facilitates mutually profitable transactions
   4. Service that earns customer loyalty
   5. Operations that scale with economic cycles
   6. Finance that controls cash flow and funds the future
   7. Culture that upholds a unique brand experience

❑ Branding is:
   1. A customer experience that
   2. They value
   3. They willingly pay for
   4. They want to repeat
   5. Not available elsewhere
   6. They'll tell others about.

❑ Culture overrules business rules and KPIs. What is your culture and how is it impacting your business operations?

❑ Understand the pillars and the KPIs used to manage and improve the business.

❑ Implement business rules with I.T. for each of the pillars to enforce the rules and scale the company.

Ask Yourself

❑ Where do I need to improve my business acumen? What will I do to make those improvements.

❑ What level of business acumen do I have on staff? Where do I need to make improvements?

❑ What is my culture? How do I want this to change?

❑ Can I offer my customers insights and best practices for implementing the KPIs and business rules in their organization?

Ask Your Team

❑ What is your level of business acumen for your part of our operation?

❑ Where do you think we can improve to create a better, more valuable company?

❑ How would you describe our culture?

❑ How do you think our customers describe our culture?

❑ How can we change our culture to better serve our target customers?

Action Plan

❑ Formalize your culture statement if you don't have one.

❑ Identify your KPIs for each of the seven business pillars.

❑ Check your business rules against those KPIs.

❑ Implement the business rules for your organization so that you can illustrate best business practices to your customers.

❑ Consider up-leveling your business and executive acumen. Check out http://ExecutiveStrategySummit.com.

Chapter 9:
Pivot Factor –
From Trusted Technology Advisor
to Trusted Business Partner

Reseller partners in the I.T. industry strive to become a trusted advisor in the hopes that customers choose to seek out their counsel. While this seems admirable, it's short sighted. An advisor gets pigeon-holed in to a technology niche, usually one that's tactical. This is where MSPs often get stuck.

A much better position is that of a trusted business partner, one who is considered strategic, understanding the big picture and able to direct technical resources to achieve business objectives. When selling complex, mission critical technology, customers must trust you before they'll commit the future of their company into the hands of your team.

What's More Important: Transaction of Trust?

What's more important in sales? The transaction or customer trust?

How you and your team answer this question determines if you see sales actions as being short term or long term. That viewpoint decides how your business grows, how long it will last, and ultimately how rich you become.

IS YOUR BUSINESS A TRANSACTION ENGINE OR A TRUST ENGINE?

I recommend focusing on building customer trust knowing the transactions flow from your earned position of a trusted vendor, trusted technology advisor, and ultimately a trusted business partner.

What's the Business Difference?

A transaction fills your belly and pays the bills today. Trust lines up business for tomorrow and the future.

A transaction helps you meet today's quota (how the sales boss chooses to measure performance). Trust puts business capital in the emotional bank account.

A transaction means you win. Trust mean you both you and your customer win.

A transaction means they traded money for something. Trust means you both traded up for more of everything.

A transaction sets the current spending limit of your customer. Trust sets the customer's future spending limit.

A transaction has a beginning and an end. Trust has a beginning and can go on forever.

A transaction sets the ceiling on how far a customer will go with you. Trust removes that ceiling: the more trust, the higher the ceiling.

How Do You Measure Trust?

It's easy to measure transactions: we count the number of customers and count the dollars. Measuring trust is bit more challenging.

> TRUST IS AN ATTRIBUTION. PEOPLE HAVE TO SAY, "I TRUST YOU."

The moment you ask, "How much do you trust me?" the data gets skewed. While pollsters will ask questions like, "What's your trust level?" and then offer a scale from no trust to complete trust, how can you trust the answer?

Trust is best measured under duress. When something goes wrong, you know if you can trust or not. It's that clear cut, there's either trust or no trust.

Same thing happens with customers. In times of trouble, they call the one they trust most. When they're in an emergency situation, you'll know they trust you because they're calling for help.

By the same token, you earn trust quickest during difficult times. That's why complaining customers present you with the opportunity to generate valuable business capital when you choose to engage with them, converting their complaints into trust.

Trust is Earned

You can't generate trust by saying, "Trust me!" That phrase causes people to question trust, not increase it. Stop saying that.

The biggest trust creator is consistency: the experience customers can expect time after time. Ultimately, a consistent experience becomes your brand, whether personal or corporate.

Trust is most quickly earned under duress. That's why the military uses boot camps to craft comradery, an intimate form of trust, and why fraternities haze pledges.

While you don't have the luxury to cause customers duress, you can respond to their stressful situations and become the hero, creating commensurate trust.

If you think about it, when customers come to you, they already have a certain level of trust that you can solve the problem that's their top priority. It's up to you to deliver.

Trust Comes from Performance

A psychologist once told me that it takes eleven positive events to overcome a single negative event. This means you must build up many positive situations to create trust. Your customers can only trust you after they see personal evidence of trustworthy behavior.

This means you have to perform to gain trust. Show up on time: get a trust point. Deliver your proposal on time: gain a trust point. Keep your word: gain a trust point. Be viewed as having integrity: gain a trust point. When you perform to the expectations you set with your customer, you get a trust point. Miss that expectation and you lose eleven points.

This idea extends to you using what you sell. Customers expect you to actually use the technology you're selling to run your business. Use what you sell, gain a trust point.

For this reason, the first technology sale is to yourself. All vendors must offer not for resale (NFR) products to their re-sellers and make that deployment successful.

> YOUR BEST PRODUCT ENDORSEMENT IS A SALES TEAM
> WHO EATS THEIR OWN COOKING.

When the Chips are Down, Amplify Trust

You can gain many, many points if you can deliver in an emergency. This is a *critical trust event*.

Let's say that your customer has to get a new product on line in the next 24 hours. With your help, you can get them going. You have concert tickets to see your favorite band perform their farewell tour this evening. What do you do? You get to choose.

If you forgo the show (give the tickets to another customer and you get double points) and get your customer on line, you've just generated 100 trust points. And if you play your cards right, you might get the boss to pay for you to travel to catch the next stop on the show tour. (It's happened!)

Guard Trust Like It's Solid Gold

Do everything you can to bank all the trust points you can. This means you can't take your eye off the ball. A few moments of inattention and you can destroy all that work you've done. This is why sales professionals don't like to take vacations. (Although if you create backup systems, you can.)

When you create, protect, and expand trust in your customers, your competitors don't have a chance.

Chapter Summary

❑ Trust is more important than a transaction in a recurring revenue business model.

❑ You earn trust through consistency, tough conversations, and successfully facing challenges.

❑ Do everything in your power to protect trust because it is your prime business asset.

Ask Yourself

❑ How does my culture support the development, protection, and expansion of trust?

❑ Where can I make improvements to actively improve customer trust?

❑ Given that we must earn trust, how can I ensure that this is a key performance indicator for my business?

Ask Your Team

❑ Where do you detect areas that create trust issues with our prospects and customers?

❑ When you think that we're going to damage customer trust, what do you do about it?

❑ Do you realize that when you're talking to our customers, you're potentially reaching up three levels in their organization? What can you do to be more presentable, valuable, and trustworthy to the top level of our customers?

Action Plan

❑ Monitor customer trust.

❑ Work with your team to build, protect, and deepen trust.

❑ Make customer trust a key part of your culture.

Chapter 10:
Pivot Factor –
Start at the Top

Traditionally, I.T. has been sold to the data center and that's now pivoting to where I.T. is sold to every department.

In this new business model environment, it makes way more sense and becomes much easier to start the conversation at the top.

Read on to discover why this is the case and how to identify the players who have low resistance to selling, how to start a conversation with them, and then how to extend the conversation to the other players who have higher sales resistance.

You're Selling Three Levels Up

When you sell complex, high-consideration products, you're selling up the executive chain of command by two to three levels, sometimes more. You'll be selling to the top of the organization and ultimately the board of directors because I.T. is the mission-critical engine that runs virtually every business.

> AN EXECUTIVE WILL NEVER BRING INTO THEIR INNER CIRCLE SOMEONE WHO MIGHT BE RISKY OR EMBARRASSING.

An executive will never engage with someone who they believe will embarrass them or make poor recommendations because it's a reflection on their judgement. It's not worth the risk to their career.

For this reason, you've got to dress to their level, use language of their level, research what they think about, read, and pay attention to. You've got to mirror their reality if you're going to be a part of their reality.

Unfortunately, some executives may not appreciate a Millennial's dress style, word choice, behavior, obsession with their mobile device, piercings and tattoos, and so may exclude them from their inner circle. They may not welcome their language patterns, including words such as like, cool, and gross. While it's not fair, it is what is for now.

Does your sales team have the skills, insights, vocabulary, and personal image to be invited to converse at those levels?

If not, you're losing sales to a more well-regarded competitor, regardless of your product quality.

What Do You Say When You Get There?

Sales people work hard to get an executive audience yet often put little effort into developing the message and practicing the delivery for when they get the meeting. Most sales professionals stumble during executive conversations, overshadow the excellence of their offering and leave big deals on the table.

In a study by the *Economist*, 71 percent of executives surveyed indicated that they found commercial messages unattractive and unappealing in what's purported to be informational content.[38] You've got to come into the conversation prepared, knowing what they find relevant, valuable, and insightful.

Here are five strategies to make your executive discussions effective.

1. Ask Smarter Questions

So many canned sales questions are "Hey, stupid…" questions such as "Would you like to save 50 percent on your operating costs?" They figure, only an idiot would say, "No, we're looking forward to increasing our operating expenses."

The question is manipulative, extracts no meaningful information, kills dialog, and makes the questioner look like a dope.

---

[38] http://www.missingthemark.ads.economist.com/presentation

And yet, almost every sales hack asks the question. You, personally might want a tongue-in-cheek answer ready the next time you're asked this question, such as, "No, we are only interested in saving 100 percent. Can you do that?"

A much better way to make the same point is, "Our customers have discovered that they can typically slash operating costs by 50 percent with the method I propose to discuss with you. Is this something that you'd like to explore?"

Notice that we introduce the savings by reporting success that you've already achieved with other customers, which increases your credibly and makes your assertion inarguable. Success stories and third-party endorsements increase your persuasiveness and make your claims stick. This combination decreases resistance to your message.

A common sales question: "What keeps you up at night?" USA Today interviewed 10 Fortune 500 CEOs, asking that question. Nine responded with, "Nothing, I'm working on my vision." One told the truth: "My teenage daughter."

A much better question: "What prevents your team from achieving your vision and mission?"

2. Talk Efficiently

You only have to tell an executive something once. They are expert at rapidly grasping the facts, required for their position. When they need more information, they'll ask. Practice your discussion to clearly and quickly make your point.

> IF YOU FIND YOURSELF SAYING, "LIKE I SAID..." TO AN EXECUTIVE, YOU'RE BLOWING IT.

Use the BLOT concept (Bottom Line On Top) when talking with executives. This means starting with your provable, relevant conclusion and then move through the supporting rationale. If you attempt to lead executives through the data to a conclusion, you will create resistance that may result in dismissal before you've made your key point.

3. Talk Articulately

Record your practice presentation (you are rehearsing for the big moment, aren't you?) and listen critically to your performance. Notice how many verbal fillers are you using, such as: like, OK, you know, um, at the end of the day, net-net, bottom line, and other hackney, overused non-words.

Practice again leaving out the fluff and fillers. Practice again until you can deliver your presentation cleanly.

Here's why this is important: executives will never consider someone that would embarrass them in front of their peers or board of directors. This means that you must be polished and professional in diction and discussion if you want access to the inner sanctum.

4. Deliver Real Thought Leadership

My colleague, Jeannine Edwards once asked, "What's the statute of limitations on thought leadership?" The answer, "This conversation."

> THOUGHT LEADERSHIP IS AN ATTRIBUTION.
> YOU CAN'T CREDIBLY CLAIM IT.

Executives value integrity and intelligence. You can't fake either of those for long. Nor can you claim them: these are characteristics that are attributed to you after consistently demonstrating them. Similarly, you can't claim that you are a though leader, innovative, nor disruptive. Others must say those things about you.

Most sales professionals aspire to be trusted partners, that position is earned by bringing fresh ideas and insights to every meeting. Executives won't bring a sales pro into their inner circle until that person can consistently show value to the exec's organization and career.

> EXECUTIVES GRAVITATE TO RELEVANT THOUGHT LEADERSHIP, SO DELIVER FRESH, SIGNIFICANT IDEAS IN EVERY CONVERSATION.

You can develop thought leadership by watching other thought leaders and using them for inspiration. Start forecasting what will happen in your industry and hone your skills to identify trends that have impact on your customer's business. Read new ideas daily and develop your talking points, keeping them fresh.

> THE THREE ELEMENTS OF EXECUTIVE SALES SUCCESS:
> 1) REPETITIVE RELEVANCE
> 2) EXPANDING VALUE
> 3) UNSHAKABLE TRUST.

Use these ideas – and practice – so that when you speak with executives, you become a respected top-producing sales professional and business advisor who consistently delivers thought leadership.

5. Communicate to Match Executive Temperament

An executive's temperament determines how they think about the organization and therefore drives how they make decisions. Each executive role has a different set of objectives, priorities, and criteria that facilitates their job. Each has a unique viewpoint of what represents value, has a different view on risk, and unique motivators that drive their behaviors.

Key performance indicators (KPIs) measure what's important for an executive to keep their job. When the KPI is high, their job is safe. When the KPI is low, they go, right now! KPIs drive all temperament, ultimately determining a person's suitability for their role.

Selling to the C Suite

In every technology sale, there are at least three players: the CIO, the CFO, and the CEO. In government and education, the CEO is represented by the agency chief, general, chief of staff, admiral, mayor, governor, superintendent, dean, provost, etc.

When other departments are involved, you may include the chief revenue officer (CRO), the chief operating officer (COO), and the chief human resources officer (CHRO). You may also run across the chief information security officer (CISO), legal team, and others that may be involved in making sure that all business rules are represented.

When working with healthcare, we must also consider the clinical side of the operation, beyond the scope of this book.

Round up the agreement of the CEO, CFO, and CIO, and you often have the support you need to do business.

Why It's Hard to Sell Technology to the Data Center

Have you ever noticed that selling to I.T. is difficult? They're highly resistant to sales calls. They don't like to talk about new technologies. They're highly skeptical about anything that they haven't experienced.

At first glance, this might be surprising given that they tend to be geeks who love new technology. Isn't that what attracted them to I.T. in the first place?

While a new data center team member may start out enthusiastic about exploring technology, they very quickly learn that new technology causes issues when you're responsible to keep the system up and running. They soon become highly resistant to change because it creates risk of downtime and puts their career in jeopardy.

CIO Temperament Overview

A CIO's KPI is one thing, and one thing only: *uptime*. As long as the system is up, running well, and secure, so is their career. If the system goes down resulting in major business impact, their career is over.

Keep this in mind as you converse with the CIO because for this reason, they are *risk averse*, avoiding anything that might cause a security or system issue. Every new technology requires a proof of concept and a meticulous deployment strategy.

The CIO's role is the *tactical* deployment of business systems, focusing on *how* to achieve the outcome and *who* will do the job.

Their planning timeframe tends to be short, a year or less, because many of them operate in a reactive mode only planning for the next annual budget cycle. While some CIOs plan for longer time spans, they tend to be the exception.

They can only *spend* their budget, having to solicit approval for any expenditure above their signature limit. The only way they get more money is in an emergency, and that's likely to be a career-limiting event.

Their role is to *curate* and *manage* the data, with no real caring about the data itself.

> In a cloud world, CIO might stand for Career Is Over.
> It should stand for Change In Orientation.

Therefore, they want to know that the data and system is *safe*, and therefore they're safe. To do this requires *visibility* into all aspects of the data systems, both under their direct control and outsourced services.

What they'd prefer to do is *innovate*, yet this is almost impossible without executive air cover and a sandbox that allows them to safely play with new technologies.

They like to feel *invisible*. I got this insight at 36,000 feet from the CIO of a large pharmaceutical company with data centers in 65 countries. After four glasses of red wine in first class, he revealed to me that his top goal was being invisible. "When they notice me, I'm in trouble," he lamented.

Is it any wonder that CIOs have **high resistance** to new technology and don't find attractive many of the value propositions of current technology? It's just not worth the career risk to consider anything that's not tried and true. Better to start your conversation elsewhere.

CFO Temperament Overview

CFOs have two KPI's: *cash flow* and *compliance*. While you may be thinking that their KPIs are profit, return on investment, total cost of ownership, and watching budgets, none of these things get them fired. A major CFO function is historical, reporting what other departments have done, and there's little career risk in that.

CFOs spend every business day considering *cash flow* thinking, "Can I pay my vendors and meet payroll?" If they can't, they're fired — along with everyone else.

Their second KPI is *compliance*: are the financials GAAP (generally accepted accounting principles) compliant? Have tax documents been filed on time? Are they in compliance with government mandates (SEC, Sarbanes Oxley, etc.) and all other regulatory demands?

Today, it's not just the CFO's career that's on the line because the penalties for being out of compliance can be egregious: they can go to jail.

> FOR MODERN DAY CFOS, ROI STANDS FOR RISK OF INCARCERATION. THEY TELL ME THAT THEY DON'T LOOK GOOD IN ORANGE.

They're responsible for directing the funding *sequence*, allocating funds by the month or quarter, directing *when, where,* and *how much* money becomes available. Their planning timeframe tends to be one to two years out, several budget cycles. The exception to the rule is when planning for real estate and multi-year capital investments.

CFOs are *risk aware*, willing to consider risk/reward payoffs. While they'll choose the conservative route, with the right guarantees and assurances, insurance and due diligence, they'll take a calculated risk.

When it comes to budgets, they're responsible for *auditing* how people spend the money within business rules. They consider the cash flow impact of a purchase as much, if not more than the overall cost and ROI.

When it comes to data, their job is to *create* and *mine* data, generating reports for the CEO. To make this happen they want to make sure that they're working with *accurate* data and can extract *insight* because the CFO's role is to support the CEO's vision and provide the cash flow *control* and future funding to make it happen. Some CFOs are called comptrollers, business controllers, or financial controllers, reflecting this role of control.

They make decisions based on being *comfortable*. You've probably heard CFOs say, "I'm not comfortable with this." Or, "I'm comfortable with these numbers."

The CFO's temperament means they have *medium resistance* to sales conversations and new ideas. If your value proposition upgrades cash flows and compliance, start the conversation here.

CEO Temperament Overview

The CEO's KPI is *mission accomplished*.

For a commercial business executive, the mission is increasing shareholder value, determined by the business model and some blend of *profit* and *growth*. When highly profitable, they don't have to grow much, and conversely, if they are growing like crazy they don't have to make much profit.

In government and education, it's about accomplishing the mission that's been mandated for the organization or agency.

Their role is **strategic**, bounded by the organization's *what* objective and *why* rationale under the guidance of the Board of Directors or their superiors.

CEOs have the longest planning timeframe in the organization, looking three to five years, or more, into the future.

CEOs search for improvements in *efficiency* because this allows them to increase profits for the same level of sales and grow without additional capital investment, or accomplish their mission with fewer resources.

Today, *flexibility* becomes extremely important to adapt and adjust to rapidly changing market conditions and fluctuating demands of government and education.

> **A CEO** CREATES A FUTURE THAT DOES NOT EXIST
> USING METHODS THAT HAVE NOT YET BEEN INVENTED.

A CEO's risk profile shows that they can **accept risk** because they are creating a future that does not exist using methods that have not yet been invented. Risk averse executives don't last long in today's chaotic business conditions, they're outrun and outgunned by those who can manage, mitigate, and profit from risk.

They set budgets by orchestrating their resources to accomplish their mission. Show them how they can better, faster, and safer accomplish their mission and they'll set a budget for you.

They *consume* data to make executive decisions around how to best achieve their objectives, *monetization* for commercial organizations and *mission accomplished* for government and education.

They want *topsight* (the 30,000-foot view of where they are) and *foresight* (where they want to go) to make intelligent and defensible decisions, relying on data provided by the rest of their team.

EVEN THE BEST GPS CAN'T OFFER GUIDANCE UNTIL IT KNOWS WHERE YOU ARE AND WHERE YOU WANT TO GO.

They want to feel *confident* about their decisions in the face of rapidly changing market and field conditions.

In summary, the CEO has *low resistance* to new ideas and new technology. They are willing to consider disruptive technology when it delivers an outcome that advances their mission. Start your conversation with the CEO and if they're impressed, they'll connect you with everybody you need to know to get the deal done.

Title Domain	Objectives			Priorities				Criteria		
	KPIs	Role	Time Frame (years)	Risk	Budget	Data	Know	Do	Feel
CIO Data	Uptime	Tactical: How & Who	0-1	Averse	Spend	Curate, Manage	Safe, Visibility	Innovate	Invisible
CFO Money	Cash flow, Compliance	Sequence: Where, When, & How Much	1-2	Aware	Audit	Create, Mine	Insight, Accurate	Control	Comfortable
CEO Vision	Mission Accomplished Profit & Growth	Strategic: What & Why	3-5	Accept	Set	Consume, Monetize	Topsight, Foresight	Decide	Confident

Executive Temperament Regulates Acceptance of, or Resistance to New Technology
(Key: **Low Resistance**, Some Resistance, *High Resistance*)

What Executives Need to Feel to Say Yes

You've probably heard that people buy based on emotion and justify based on fact or logic. You may have questioned that observation. Here's evidence that it's true.

The right most column of the Executive Temperament Matrix, above, hints at what executives must *feel* to agree to your proposal. When they do a gut check before deciding, this is the feeling they want to notice, and they know it when they feel it. The desired feeling is different for each executive role, and is probably different than what you want to feel.

To win, you must provide the experience and data that triggers the feeling each executive needs to make their decision.

Why All I.T. Gets Bought

Summarizing the KPIs of the technology committee, the only reasons why the executive team approves an I.T. purchase is because it contributes to uptime, cash flow, compliance, mission accomplished, profit and growth.

> EXECUTIVES ONLY PURCHASE I.T. TO SUPPORT THEIR KPIS.
> THERE ARE NO OTHER REASONS.

When your value propositions and proposals embrace the technology committee's KPIs, you'll succeed. Miss any of them and they reject your recommendation.

CIOs Need Your Help

When a CIO asks you for a *proposal*, they are asking for help persuading the rest of the technology committee to agree with their decision. The CIO is sold but needs help convincing their counterparts. If they could buy with their signature authority, they would ask you for a *quote* instead. More about this on page 63.

> AN RFP IS A CRY FOR HELP TO CONVINCE THE APPROVAL COMMITTEE,
> OTHERWISE THEY'D ASK FOR AN RFQ.

Yet most MSPs write a detailed proposal for the CIO, ignoring the decision criteria and requirements of the CFO and CEO. This slows down the process and creates more problems than it solves.

Help the CIO present compelling evidence that the rest of the executive team needs to feel comfortable and confident about the recommendation.

Better yet, have direct conversations with the rest of the technology committee to help round up support by discussing how your proposal supports the executive team's KPIs.

Why CIOs Don't Want You Talking with the Executive Team

No doubt, you've had CIOs forbid you from talking to their executives. In fact, old school sales strategies demanded that you recruit a "coach" to help you navigate the executive level.

I reject this approach. Why would you want to abdicate your relationship to someone who doesn't understand psychology and technology like you do? You can have a meeting with anyone you desire.[39] There are very good reasons for you to conduct the conversation, given that the CIO doesn't regard important business value propositions the same way as the rest of the executive team.

Here's why CIOs don't want you to talk to their team. In the past, certain vendors (you know who they are) have gone over their head and persuaded the CEO to take a certain action that ran counter to the CIO's desires. These vendors did this because it works.

---

[39] Stu Heinecke wrote the book about this, *How to Get a Meeting with Anyone.* http://amzn.to/2kGQRzZ

> ## CIOs WHO HAVE BEEN THROWN UNDER THE BUS BY VENDORS WON'T LET THAT HAPPEN AGAIN.

To access the technology committee through the CIO, you have to illustrate that you are supportive and safe, holding their best interests in mind. Do this by discussing the past and promise a new future. Consider this script:

"I know that a purchase like this demands careful consideration by your executive team for their approval. I have experience in successfully presenting this to executives in a short, non-technical, business-focused conversation.

"I propose that we review the presentation and that you schedule 30 minutes for me with your execs.

"It's one less thing that you have to prepare and you can position me as the business expert and you as the technology expert. And if they say no, they shoot me down, not you."

Then ask them, "Who will be reviewing this and what do they need to say yes to the proposal? Will you work with me to build the business case to make sure that you get what you want from the approval committee?"

Now you're establishing valuable relationships with all decision makers and substantially improving your sales success.

Chapter Summary

- ❑ Each executive in the C-suite has a different role, responsibility, and temperament. Understand these and your conversations will always be relevant and meaningful.
- ❑ An executive's KPIs drive their temperament, so align your value propositions to support their individual KPIs for maximum impact.
- ❑ All I.T. is purchased to support executive KPIs.
- ❑ Executives seek a specific gut feeling that lets them know they've made the best decision. For them to say yes, you must deliver the experiences and data to create that feeling.

- ❑ The CIO has the highest resistance to sales and new technologies, the CEO has the lowest resistance. Begin new conversations with the CEO for the fastest results.
- ❑ Help the CIO get what they want by co-creating proposals that present the evidence that aligns with the executive team's KPIs to persuade the CFO, CEO, and anyone else that needs to say yes.

Ask Yourself

- ❑ How well does the executive temperament overview align with my organizational experience?
- ❑ How does my view need to change to optimize success when engaged in executive conversations?
- ❑ How can I improve our proposal process to better help executives make a defensible decision?

Ask Your Team

- ❑ How do we prepare proposals for the technology approval committee?
- ❑ How can we improve our success when working with technology purchase committees?
- ❑ What CIOs do you know who would introduce us to their executives? If not, why not?

Action Plan

- ❑ Consider executive temperament in all discussions.
- ❑ Change your executive proposal process and format.
- ❑ Check in with your executive friends to confirm and augment your knowledge about decision criteria and process.

Chapter 11:
Pivot Factor –
Master Seven Critical
Executive Sales Skills

Sales leadership isn't just the ability to attract good customers and direct good people, it's the intention and skills required to operate a sustainable, scalable, profitable business. The more complex and high consideration your offering, the more leadership skills you need for success because you're selling to sophisticated and savvy executives.

Ninety percent of commercial CEOs come from a sales background.[40] This means that executives have personally used every trick in the sales book. Don't ever use the manipulative sales strategies frequently taught by sales trainers whose thought leadership expired decades ago.

> NINETY PERCENT OF COMMERCIAL CEOS HAVE A SALES BACKGROUND. THEY'VE USED EVERY CLOSE YOU'LL TRY ON THEM.

Your leadership success doesn't hinge on how much you know, but how well you get along and play well with others.

"Eighty five percent of your financial success is due to your personality and ability to communicate, negotiate, and lead. Shockingly, only 15 percent is due to technical knowledge" according to the Study of Engineering Education, Charles Riborg Mann, published in 1918 by the Carnegie Foundation. What makes this century-old observation interesting is

---

[40] Reported in Anthony Parinello's excellent book, *Selling to Vito* http://amzn.to/2y8Kqbn

that it's still true today. It was shocking then because the assumption was product knowledge is the source of success. While it's a component, it's not enough.

In working with sales professionals of all types over the past three decades, I've identified seven skills required for sustainable success selling to executives. When one skill is weak or missing, sales trouble follows, sooner or later. The good news: these skills can be developed and improved.

What follows is a discussion of the executive skill stack. Like application developers and programmers must have a skill stack to create valuable, effective, and usable code, an executive must have certain skills to run a sustainable, scalable, profitable, and ultimately salable organization.

Read on to identify if you have these skills and to assess where you need to enhance them.

1. Presence

Presence is that certain something that attracts people, commands their attention, and permits a leader to engage. Presence is the ultimate in first impressions. Without it, you don't even get a chance to sell, even when you have a position of authority.

Presence is a powerful combination of emotional intelligence (EQ) plus integrity that creates charisma.

> BEING A SMART JERK WON'T MAKE YOUR CAREER.

According to organizational researchers, 35 percent of your success is because of your EQ and 50 percent because of your cognitive capacity (IQ), and 15 percent is your knowledge. Emotional intelligence is the ability to balance your awareness and management of yourself, others, and things.

When you're unaware of others, you're a narcissist. When you're unaware of things, you're a minimalist. When you're unaware of yourself, you're an altruist. A successful sales professional must be present to and balance their awareness.

Without integrity, you're doomed. Once customer executives and your team discover that you're not of your word, the game is over, forever. You've blown your trust.

Ask yourself: On a scale of one to ten, how is your ability to balance your awareness? Which awareness requires attention?

2. Discipline

While we'd love to be free spirits, unbound by convention and routine, that doesn't work for a sales executive.

Discipline requires personal and professional routines. It's within that structure that we truly find freedom to focus on the variables that sales executives manage.

For example, Steve Jobs, arguably one of the most effective and disruptive businessmen, wore a uniform of black mock turtleneck, blue jeans, and New Balance sneakers. This meant he had one less thing to think about. He also had a meditation practice that kept him centered and effective.

> THE MAIN THING IS TO KEEP THE MAIN THING THE MAIN THING.
> – STEPHEN COVEY

Without a personal routine, you'll skip meals, not get enough sleep, and not get the exercise you need, all of which impact your most valuable resource, your cognitive capacity.

Without a disciplined sales routine, you'll fight fires all day long and never attend to the critical account strategy, pipeline prioritization, and customer maintenance that is the hallmark of an effective sales executive.

Ask yourself: Does your daily routine support you for being your most resourceful? Does your routine ensure that every aspect of your territory gets attention?

3. Foresight

When was the last time you did a future vision exercise? If it wasn't within the past thirty days, you may face a looming disaster and don't yet see it.

Why? Because, as Scott Adams puts it, "Goal thinkers only see what's between them and the goal line. Systems thinkers avoid slow moving problems." Scott points out the big difference between being tactical, working to the goal, and being strategic, creating a system that scores goals.[41]

Your executive customers have a long-range vision of the future and you've got to be able to go there with them, as well as lead them there with your I.T. foresight.

> THE STUMBLING BLOCK WHEN SELLING TO EXECUTIVES IS THE MISMATCH OF THE SALES PERSON'S SHORT-TERM VIEW AND THE EXECUTIVE'S LONG-TERM VIEW OF THE FUTURE.

Foresight is how we engineer our sales systems that generate value for our customers. We must be looking forward beyond their horizon if we are to deliver value that's consistent, sustainable, scalable, and profitable.

Ask yourself: What is your vision horizon? If it's not at least three years out, you're on a downward path. When was the last time you revisited your vision? If it's not in the last thirty days, you're developing a blind spot.

4. Business Acumen

Most sales people have a strong skill set in one area of business acumen, sales. If you're selling a low-consideration product with a short sales cycle, that may be enough.

---

[41] Read Scott Adam's excellent book, *How to Fail at Almost Everything and Still Win Big* http://amzn.to/2y8KcRq

Yet if you're selling a high-consideration, complex product involving multiple decision makers, you need to understand how their business works and map the product to their business roadmap. You need business acumen to understand their motivations and how to satisfy their needs.

A successful sales executive understands the elements of business so that they can speak the language of every player in the organization. Without business acumen, you'll always be viewed as a sales person. With business acumen, you'll be viewed as a trusted business partner. I discussed this in more detail on page 63. Here's a synopsis below:

The Seven Business Pillars

1. **Products** that create unique value for the target market
2. **Marketing** that triggers relevant conversations
3. **Sales** that facilitates mutually profitable transactions
4. **Service** that earns customer loyalty
5. **Operations** that scale with economic cycles
6. **Finance** that controls cash flow and funds the future
7. **Culture** that upholds a unique brand experience

Ask yourself: On a scale of one to 10, how proficient are you at each of the seven business pillars? Where do you need to improve your acumen? How can you get tutoring in the elements of that pillar?

5. Communication Skills

A successful sales executive must be able to communicate ideas and actions clearly, aligned with how their customer is receiving communication, and judiciously use humor. I've found that most sales breakdowns are rooted in lack of communication skills or the inability to adjust communication styles to the person and product at hand.[42]

Successful sales executives take responsibility to communicate in the way that works for the people to whom they're selling. It's often different than their natural way of communication.

Each role in your customer organization requires a different approach to processing information. For example, a CFO needs to be detail oriented and by the rules, and the marketing team wants to be flexible and creative. They each require a different approach to communication and conversation in the sales process.

> SPEAK AND WRITE WELL BECAUSE CLEAR COMMUNICATION HAS MORE VALUE THAN ANY PHYSICAL TASK YOU CAN DO.

For example, when asked, "How does it work?" there are times to say, "It works great!", a classic sales response, and there are times when you've got to deliver the nitty-gritty details. Being specific when your customer wants the big picture incites boredom, so err on the side of less detail. If they want specifics, they'll ask for more information.

Ask yourself: How often do you have problems with your customer "getting" your message? If it's more than rarely, it's time to work on your understanding of how people communicate.

6. Persuasion Skills

To sell profitably, you must persuade customers to align their priorities with your priorities and sell at prices higher than

---

[42] While a conversation about communication styles is beyond the scope of this book, you can learn more about this in my book, *Selling Disruption.* http://SellingDisruption.com

they initially want to pay because of the increase in value that you deliver. This requires persuasion and negotiating skills and the ability to create agreements that all involved want to keep.

Executives negotiate every day: with vendors, employees, bankers, customers, lawyers, politicians, and each other. The better you can negotiate, the better you can profitably run your business.

> THE BEST NEGOTIATIONS END WITH AN AGREEMENT
> THAT BOTH SIDES WANT TO KEEP.

Ask yourself: How frequently do you find yourself agreeing to things that you really don't want? How often do you think that you could have kept more margin and the other party would still be happy? How often do you feel that you could have been more persuasive? If it's not rare, consider a course in negotiation skills or learn persuasion skills. [43]

7. Makes Resourceful Decisions

Successful sales executives are comfortable with uncertainty. They initiate actions without knowing the complete roadmap because they have a decision-making system based on business rules that leads to more resourceful decisions than bad decisions.

> EXECUTIVES HAVE MORE ON THEIR TO THINK LIST
> THAN THEIR TO DO LIST.

---

[43] For more on the topic, see my book, *Guerrilla Negotiating* written to provide the antidote for the dirty tricks customers use to take the profit out of your deals. http://amzn.to/2iyFt4S

The result is efficient allocation and management of resources, such as time, personal energy, imagination, people, and money. Resourceful decisions are based on a combination of the prior six skills discussed here, plus a decision strategy that effectively considers the elements of the decision. The best sales executives use a check list to ensure that the critical elements get considered during the sales process.

You might be thinking, "I use my gut to make decisions." This isn't scalable, because you can't teach others your gut method like you can with a decision check list. Your gut is the final test, not the only test.

Ask yourself: Do you have a decision-making checklist, one that you routinely use and refine? If not, time to build it.

How Did You Do?

Be honest with yourself, as you're the only person to benefit. Now that you've identified where you need to build your executive sales strengths, put together your personal plan to make it happen.[44]

Chapter Summary

- ❑ When working with executives, you've got to understand their challenges and opportunities as business leaders.
- ❑ You'll gain the respect of business leaders when you can exhibit the key skills of leadership.
- ❑ Routinely assess your leadership skills, upgrading the ones where you need to grow.

---

[44] If you want to work on your skills, consider attending the Executive Strategy Skills Summit. Specifically for Executives, upgrade your strategic skills and leave with a Monday-ready action plan. http://ExecutiveStrategySummit.com

Ask Yourself

- ❑ How complete is my leadership skill stack?
- ❑ What do I need to improve to better relate to my executive customers?
- ❑ What's my personal leadership improvement plan?
- ❑ How can I lead my team to better leadership skills?

Ask Your Team

- ❑ How do you consider yourself in terms of leadership?
- ❑ Would you be interested in developing those skills?
- ❑ What might hold you back from being a leader, both in your team, in your community, and with our customers?

Action Plan

- ❑ Make leadership skills development as important as product knowledge.
- ❑ Identify the leadership skills in your team and develop them.
- ❑ Share leadership skills concepts with your customers.

Chapter 12:
Pivot Factor –
Your Sales Compensation Plan

The traditional approach to selling I.T. has been to use commissioned sales people to find the deals. They hunt new customers – often referred to as *logos* – and earn commission based on the purchases of that customer. They stay involved in managing the customer relationship and direct the company resources.

In the days of just selling customers a PC with no additional services required, this made sense. As the solution complexity increases, this sales system becomes much less effective.

> WITH TODAY'S COMPLEX I.T. SYSTEMS, WE MUST SEPARATE
> BUSINESS DEVELOPMENT FROM TECHNICAL DEPLOYMENT.

Here's the big challenge: while the sales team attempts look after the needs of their accounts, they don't have time or energy to find new customers, nor the time to keep up with the technical learning curve needed to serve customers well. When working with both complex products and multiple decision makers, they just can't do a good job of both sales and customer service. This must change for your company to be efficient and effective.

Traditional Sales Compensation Models

The industry uses some mix of base pay, draw, and commission on gross profit. Because of the razor thin margins on hardware, there's often little money for decent commissions, unless higher-margin services are part of the solution mix.

What sales compensation works best? Which is fair? It depends on the sales cycle, how long a customer considers before making the commitment.

Short sales cycles and all-commission compensation work well because the salesperson can see a correlation between what they do and their paycheck. Managers can incent more sales with stretch goals.

> THE BIGGEST ISSUE IN SALES MANAGEMENT TODAY IS USING
> SHORT-CONSIDERATION SALES COMPENSATION
> FOR LONG-CONSIDERATION PROJECTS AND PRODUCTS.

Very long sales cycles work better with salaried compensation, yet there needs to be an additional success metric, such as pipeline growth or the number of prospect conversations.

Sales behavior problems show up when there's a mismatch between sales cycle time and compensation strategy.

Pivot to Business Development

In the world of Business Services Providers, the sales role moves to only finding a new prospect and initiating the relationships that lead to a business agreement. The technical diagnostics and prescriptive advice then falls on the shoulders of the technical support team, not the sales person. The sales role evolves to one of business development.

Pay Your Sales Teams to Only Sell Assessments

Want your hunters to bag new logos? Pay them to sell business technology assessments. Give them the lion's share, if not all of the assessment fee but offer them no additional commission on what's sold post assessment.

Employ your technical sales support team to execute and deliver the assessment. You'll fund them with the profits of resulting post-assessment sales. Use the recurring revenue to pay your farmers a salary to keep the customer happy and run a highly profitable, recurring revenue business.

> **WANT LOTS MORE BUSINESS RIGHT NOW? PAY YOUR BEST SALES HUNTERS FOR CLOSING BUSINESS CASE ASSESSMENTS.**

Tell your customers that the assessment team is not commissioned so that you can deliver objective results. This eliminates conflict of interest and substantially increases customer trust when they feel that the advice isn't tied to potential revenue. Most free assessments have a connection to a specific vendor so are considered questionable by savvy executives.

This strategy means commission-motivated hunters will hunt, not possible with low-commission recurring revenue sales. A hunter gets frustrated and lazy when they don't have a clear commission goal or have a fixed income.

Your hunters may not initially like this, but when you show them how to make lots more money much faster, they'll jump on the phones and sell business case assessments to CEOs.

You may find that you'll be as business as you want from a single sales professional selling two to four business case assessments per month.

While the sales, execution, and delivery of business case assessments go way beyond the scope of this book, ask your favorite vendors if they have tools of this nature and connect with the MSP to BSP community for recommendations and resources.[45]

---

[45] Details at MSPtoBSP.com

Chapter Summary

❑ Sales compensation must change to better align with the cash flows of a subscription model yet still motivate commission-driven sales people.

❑ Short sales cycle products support commissions, long sales cycle products need a salaried position to be successfully sold.

❑ Business Service Providers benefit from only compensating their sales team for finding new customers, not from products sold.

Ask Yourself

❑ How can I pivot to paying my sales team for business development versus product sales?

❑ Which of my sales team could make the pivot? Which probably won't?

❑ How do my profits change when I only compensate my sales team for selling a business assessment?

❑ What would it cost my tech delivery team to deliver business case assessments? Is this less than what I'm paying for sales compensation?

Ask Your Team

❑ If we shifted your compensation to paying for just selling new customers on a business technology assessment, how might you see your sales success improve and income increase.

Action Plan

❑ Calculate your improved cash flows from pivoting from commissioned sales compensation to business development compensation.

❑ Pilot business development with your most business savvy sales professional.

Chapter 13:
Your Pivot Plan

It's time to put your plan in action. You've considered the key points in this book. You've argued with yourself and debated your team on key trends and business issues and come to some conclusions. What's next?

Build Your Strategic Map

Create a strategic map of what you want to accomplish and why you want to accomplish it.

You can get help with this with free resources at MSPtoBSP.com, specifically the video course on building your strategy, complete with a one sheet plan. You'll need a couple of hours to go through the exercise. It's worth it.

Share this strategic map with your executive team and select portions of it with your operations team. But keep in mind, as the responsible executive, you set the direction.

> YOUR BUSINESS ISN'T A DEMOCRACY.
> EMPLOYEES DON'T GET TO VOTE ON STRATEGY.

Build Your Action Plan Sequence

Round up all of the action steps you've identified in this book. Choose a deployment timeline with milestones and KPIs. You can't do everything at once, but you can take the next step right now. This is how you'll make the transformation and stay on track.

Join the MSP to BSP Community

A journey is much more fun when you travel with others. I promise to share more ideas and insights as they become visible and look forward to you contributing from your experiences.

> "YOU CANNOT LEARN FROM EXPERIENCES YOU'RE NOT HAVING."
> – CHRIS STARK

I'll be building resources, some free and some for fee, to help you with your transformation. Sign up at MSPtoBSP.com to evolve your business as the community evolves.

Work with Your Team to Deploy

Your team is the execution engine that makes all of this work. Guide them with your new direction and challenge them to unlearn and relearn these new business models.

Some of them won't make it. Some of them will embrace this new model. Others might wait and see. Cut loose those that resist so that the wait and see group can pivot from reluctant to supportive.

The tactical deployment is an ever-moving target. You need a flexible team to make your business work well.

> SUCCESS IS NOT A MATTER OF LUCK, IT'S A MATTER OF DISCIPLINE.

When you design, document, and operate your upgraded business model, you'll now have a business with recurring revenues that is sustainable, scalable, profitable, and ultimately saleable.

Share Your Story

I can't wait to hear about your journey! Share your story with me. Yes, there will be bumps and bruises, that's part of the voyage. Many others will be traveling with you and cheering you on.

Bon Voyage!

About the Author

Mark S A Smith works with leaders to predictably grow their organization through upgraded executive skills, effective customer acquisition systems, and communication & persuasion strategies.

Executives hire him for strategic coaching, getting unstuck, and use him as a sounding board for developing new, disruptive ideas and choosing new personal and corporate directions.

Website: BijaCo.com
LinkedIn: LinkedIn.com/in/MarkSASmith
Twitter: @MarkSASmith
Email: Mark.Smith@BijaCo.com
Mobile: +1.719.440.0439

Author

Mark wrote six books and dozens of technology playbooks and sales guides targeting government, educational, healthcare and the private sector and has authored hundreds of articles.

Selling Disruption Show Host

He hosts the Selling Disruption Show, the weekly podcast for professionals whose job depends on disruptive sales and marketing, interviewing thought leaders who disrupt their markets. Many people quoted in this book appear as guests on the show.

Listen at http://SellingDisruptionShow.com

Business Man

He is an electrical engineer, media technologist, computer programmer, hardware salesman, software marketer, and business owner.

Professional Speaker

He speaks at public and corporate events delivering pragmatic ideas to grow and succeed in business. There is no canned speech. He works with you to identify the outcome your group needs and then crafts the presentation to align with your culture, your objectives, and your vision. Contact him for a conversation about speaking at your event.

Builds Business Systems

He designs and implements sales, marketing, and customer acquisition systems that find and recruit willing buyers for disruptive products. He has designed and built channel launch kits, go-to-market playbooks, partner enablement programs, marketing strategy, customer acquisition strategies, executive presentations, systems to up-level partner business acumen, and more.

Facilitates Executive Strategy Sessions

If you're like many executives in these fast and changing times, you're having challenges clarifying your corporate strategy and getting your executive team all heading the same direction. It's not that your ideas aren't good, the challenge is getting everyone on the same page. Here's a solution.

Mark S A Smith is an executive business growth strategist with deep experience in sales, marketing, and product management. He works with executives and their team to rapidly come to agreement and start executing.

Using unique, rapid executive decision-making techniques that involve all stakeholders, tapping into the team's personal motivation strategies, and using methods to safely disrupt old ways of thinking, Mark guides your team to get on track and want to stay on track to achieve your goals. And he guarantees it.

Each member of your executive team leaves the event with a "Monday-ready" action plan to deploy with their team to take the correct next steps. And you get on-going support with six months of executive coaching to troubleshoot, encourage, and hold executives accountable for their success.

Mark S A Smith facilitates a 1.5 to 3 day on-site executive strategy session (timing depends on your mission complexity) with a combination of process training and facilitated conversation about your get-to-market mission.

The deliverables include:

❑ Discussion of management tools and processes that can be used with your team to accomplish the desired outcome.

❑ Discuss the functions of product, marketing, sales, customer support, operations, finance, and culture in support of the success of this mission.

❑ Discussion of go-to-market processes, selecting the best for this mission based on advanced models.

❑ Clear definition of what success looks like for this mission.

❑ Identify key performance indicators for tracking success and indicating areas requiring attention.

❑ Identify resources available to accomplish the mission.

❑ Identify what needs to be accomplished and grounded rationale on doing so.

❑ Identify additional resources required to accomplish the mission.

❑ Create a corporate messaging and communication plan for socializing and inculcating the mission with key team members.

❑ Create a list of prioritized activities and assign responsibility for execution.

Contact Mark to discuss if this is right for your team.

Leads the Executive Strategy Skills Summit

When you can't work any harder, you must work smarter. Specifically created for profit-and-loss-responsible executives of companies, operations, or divisions from $2 million to $100 million in revenue, this 2-day event brings executive skills and insights to founders and staff who have been promoted to the executive suite.

What makes this executive event different is the holistic view of business, not just sales or marketing or leadership, but everything required to operate a sustainable, scalable, profitable, and salable business.

Key outcomes:

❑ Develop your executive skill stack — what it is, how it's radically different from a managerial skill stack, and how to intentionally develop it.

❑ Gain a deep understanding of the Seven Business Pillars™: Product, Marketing, Sales, Service, Operations, Finance, and Culture, which give you a holistic view of your business to understand the impact of strategy decisions across pillars.

❑ Master critical executive business concepts that apply to B2B and B2C, for goods and services, for commercial, non-profit, and governmental operations.

❑ Develop your own Monday-ready phased plan to improve results and sustainably and profitably grow your company.

❑ Your satisfaction is guaranteed.

Learn more at http://ExecutiveStrategySummit.com

CPSIA information can be obtained
at www.ICGtesting.com
Printed in the USA
FFHW01n2003180718
47485405-50777FF